MW01629823

100 WONDERS in the WORLD of TORAH

ZEV T. GERSHON

Dedication

In memory of my beloved mother
Mrs. Hannah Gershon,
*whose energy and enthusiasm for life
is an example for all.*

Rabbi Yehoshua Ratner
Rosh Kollel, Nofei Aviv Community Kollel
Kislev 5785

To Whom It May Concern,

It is with great joy and admiration that I write this letter of approbation for my dear friend, Rav Zev Gershon, upon the publication of his remarkable book, "***100 Wonders in the Torah World***". Having been privileged to learn Torah with Zev daily for over 25 years, I am uniquely positioned to testify to his extraordinary qualities and the *Ahavas Torah* that infuses this work.

Zev is a person defined by his *hasmada* in learning and *emunas chachamim in Chazal*. His love for the Torah and unwavering faith in the wisdom of our sages radiate in every aspect of his life and are vividly reflected in the pages of this book. His thirst for Torah knowledge and his boundless enthusiasm to share its beauty and profundity are evident in his meticulous efforts to compile this extraordinary collection.

100 Wonders in the Torah World is a book of lists, thoughtfully designed to inspire and inform. Its easy-to-read format makes it accessible to a wide audience, while its voluminous citations ensure its depth and reliability. The work reveals not only Zev's deep reverence for chidushei Torah, but also his creative approach to presenting timeless wisdom in a way that captivates and engages the modern reader.

It is my sincere hope that ***100 Wonders in the Torah World*** will enrich the lives of its readers as profoundly as Zev has enriched mine. May this labor of love bring merit to him, his family, and all who engage with it, and may it serve as a source of illumination and inspiration for years to come.

With deep friendship and Kavod HaTorah,
Y. Ratner

Michtav Bracha

Kislev 5785

Rabbi Zev Gershon has compiled a fascinating book of more than 100 short insights on various facets of the Torah .These Torah thoughts were garnered from numerous seforim ,many of which are hard to find and in any case inaccessible to the reader not conversant in Hebrew. The compendium is full of interesting information ,some of which may not be known even to talmidei chachomim and can be an excellent resource for discussions at the Shabbos table as well as a springboard for further and deeper research .Rabbi Gershon deserves our gratitude for making these insights available. May it inspire readers to continue their growth in limud haTorah .

B'virkas HaTorah,
Yitzchak A.Breitowitz
Rav ,Kehillas Ohr Somayach
Yerushalayim

Introduction

The amount of Torah publications today is astounding. However, for people with a limited yeshiva back round, many of the astounding gems found therein have been out of reach. The purpose of this book is to introduce truly wonderous torah novelties to the English-speaking public. I am sure there will also be information here that is new even for those who have been learning Sefarim in Loshon Hakodesh. However, one needs to realize that this is only a small taste of what is out there. The reader is invited to look up the source himself and read the whole entry to learn more nuances about the topic.

Most, if not all the sources are contained in the monumental undertaking of Otzar Hachochma which has tens of thousands of Sefarim in its database. Another phenomenal source of information comes from the Responsa Project of Bar Ilan University. Their search capabilities are second to none. Finally, many Sefarim can be found at Hebrewbooks.com, or the amazing site Sefaria. When one depository might be lacking a Sefer, another one is surely available to fill the void. And given the availability of Google Translate and the Jastrow dictionary, there is no excuse for one to not access the information at its source.

Collecting this information over the years has been a labor of love. Hashem's Torah is truly amazing, and the sea of information is endless. One can also realize that sometimes it may seem that opinions are contradictory. Not to worry – "Elu VeElu Divrei Elokim Chaim", these are all part of the living Torah and we will understand the truth in all of the opinions at the end of day. I would like to thank those people who have allowed me to share this information over the years. First, the Kollel I attend in Bet Shemesh with Rabbi Yehoshua Ratner at the helm for over twenty-five years, has given me the opportunity to present the information and be challenged by it. I have shared some of the information here with our Shabbos and Yom tov guests. And therefore, my wonderful wife and family have heard the same information on multiple occasions and without complaints!

There is a tradition for the author of a Sefer to embed his name somehow in the work he has written. A 'wonder' in Hebrew is a 'Peleh" which in Gematria equals 112 with one for the Kollel of the word itself. My name Zev Tzevi is also 112 in Gematria. I hope this Sefer becomes a springboard for the reader not to only further delve into the material, but also to find other things in the many, many wonders in the World of Torah.

Contents

Swallowed up in a Cedar Tree

The prophet Yishiyahu was trying to escape from King Menashe who wanted to kill him. Yishiyahu uttered a holy name and was swallowed within a cedar tree. The servants of Menashe began sawing through the tree and when they got to Yishiyahu's mouth, he died.[1]

Yishiyahu wasn't the only one swallowed into a cedar tree. Rav Yitzchak bar Yosef consulted with a demon and was swallowed within a cedar tree. A miracle was performed for him, the tree split, and he escaped.[2]

---

1   Yevamos 49b.
2   Sanhedrin 101a

Sun – a Mark on the Wall

When the angels came to visit Avraham, one angel told him that when the sun shines through the window next year and reaches the mark on the wall he just made, Sarah would give birth to a boy.[3]

In addition, during the 10 plagues, when Moshe told Pharaoh that he would either bring a plague tomorrow, or remove a plague tomorrow, (frogs, wild beasts, pestilence, hail, or locusts), he made a mark on the wall to indicate exactly when it would happen. And when the sun shone on that mark – it took place.[4]

---

3   Tanchuma Vayera 13.
4   Sechel Tov Shmos 9:18.

The Ten Plagues – Letters

As the plagues were occurring, the Egyptians had a remarkable reminder of the plagues on their bodies – the names of the plagues were imprinted on their bodies! Either lice, wild beasts, boils, darkness, and death of the firstborn,[5] or frogs, lice, wild beasts, hail and death of the firstborn,[6] or blood, frogs and lice,[7] or blood and frogs,[8] or all ten plagues (depending on which commentary is read).[9] There is even an opinion that only the first letters of the plagues (*Detzach Adash Beachav*) were written on the foreheads of the Mitzrim at the beginning of the ten plagues and as each plague finished, that letter was erased from their foreheads.[10]

---

5   Rabbienu Ephraim Bo; Tosfos Hashalem Bo.
6   Rokeach Shmos.
7   Devarim Rabbah 7:9.
8   Tosfos Hashalem Bo.
9   Shocher Tov 78:105.
10 Vayaged Yaakov.

גיד
עד"ש
מאכם

Fire – What did Hashem show Moshe?

There were certain things that Moshe learned from Hashem, but as they say a picture is worth a thousand words. And so, Hashem showed Moshe the concepts of certain items in a display of fire – the Aron, Shulchan and Menorah,[11] or the half shekel,[12] or the kosher animals,[13] or all the work needed to build the Mishkan (depending on which commentary is read). [14]

---

11   Menachos 29a.
12   Tanchuma Ki Tisa 9.
13   Panim Yafos Shimini.
14   Lekach Tov Teruma.

Suspended in the Air

There are so many people in Jewish history that have miraculously been suspended in the air. Biblical figures include Avraham when told by Hashem to count the stars,[15] Eliezer at Lavan's house when he went to get a wife for Yitzchak,[16] the sons of Korach after the earth swallowed Korach and his followers,[17] Bilam and Pinchas during their battle,[18] or Bilam and his two sons with Tziliah from the tribe of Dan during that battle.[19]

Moshe was suspended in the air during the plague of hail,[20] and when he foretold that the plague of the firstborn would be at midnight.[21]

Bnei Yisrael were lifted off the ground at the time of Matan Torah.[22]

King David was suspended in the air as a result of Avishai.[23]

King Hiram also was suspended in the air, as he made himself out to be a G-d.[24]

After the biblical period, other notable people have been suspended in the air too, such as Rabbi Yehoshua ben Chananiah, in front of the sages of Athens,[25] Alexander the Great, to see the whole world,[26] and Rabbi Yonatan in the presence of heretics.[27]

It is not only people that have been miraculously suspended in the air. Certain objects too found themselves suspended. These include the copper snake,[28] the plague of hail after it was over,[29] Har Sinai at the

---

15 Bereishis Rabbah 44:12.
16 Yalkut Shimoni Chayeh Sarah 109.
17 Shochar Tov 46:3.
18 Tanchuma Matos 4.
19 Zohar Balak 194..
20 Rashi Vaera 9:22.
21 Chizkuni Bo 11:1..
22 Merkavat Hamishna on the Mechilta Yisro 3:7.
23 Sanhedrin 95a.
24 Midrash Hagadol Vaera; Yalkut Shimoni 367.
25 Bechoros 8b.
26 Tosfos Avoda Zara 41a.
27 Yafe Nof on Kohales Rabbah 1 [8] 4.
28 Bamidbar Rabbah 19:23.
29 Berachos 54b.

time of the giving of the Torah[30] and the keys to the Beis Hamikdash as it was being destroyed.[31] Other examples include the crown of the king of Amon,[32] the heavenly chair,[33] stones that were thrown high by the mob against Hashem,[34] and the letters of the first Luchot after they flew off.[35]

30   Shabbos 88a.
31   Shekalim 6:2.
32   Radak Divrei Hayamim 1,19:2.
33   Rashi Breishis 1:2.
34   Yalkut Shimoni Shlach 744.
35   Pesachim 87b.

The Power of Vision

As with many things, vision can be used for good or bad. There have been many times where someone has looked at another person and caused them to die. Instances include Moshe and the Egyptian,[36] Rav Sheshes and a heretic,[37] Rav Pappa and Rebbi Huna son of Rav Yehoshua gazed on Rav Chanina son of Rav Aika,[38] Rabbi Shimon on an elder and on Yehuda ben Garim,[39] Rashbi on Safra,[40] Rabbi Yochanan on a student,[41] Rav to someone who wanted to marry his daughter,[42] Abaya to the parents of Rav Pappa,[43] and the Rabbis on Rav Acha.[44] Sometimes people have gazed and burned things like the instances of Rashbi and his son who emerged from the cave,[45] and the story of Rabbi Eliezer after being banned.[46] There was also the crocodile that looked at a bird in a tree and, from fear, the birds droped into the mouth of the crocodile.[47] And the snake called an Ekase which kills with his looks.[48]

On the other hand, vision has been used for the positive, such as childbirth for the birds. There are certain birds that when they see each other and have intention to, they give birth.[49] Specifically when the male ostrich stands near the female ostrich, he stares at her and she gives birth.[50] In addition the bird named the Raah, looks at her eggs and they hatch.[51]

---

36   Yalkut Reuveini Shmos.
37   Berachos 58a.
38   Berachos 58b.
39   Shabbos 34a.
40   Yerushalmi Sheviis 9:1.
41   Baba Basra 75a.
42   Yevamos 45a.
43   Yevamos 106a.
44   Baba Basra 14a.
45   Shabbos 33b.
46   Baba Metzia 59b.
47   Madregas Haadam Bebakshes Hashleimus 17.
48   Even Shoev Balak; Yalkut Reuveini Balak.
49   Yalkut Dovid Shmini; Raza DeMeir Tazria 20.
50   Sefer Habris 14:5; Sifsei Cohen Tazria.
51   Pardes Yosef Reeh in the name of Yitav Panim on the Chagim.

The offspring can also be affected by vision as we know from Yaakov manipulating the sheep with the different wooden sticks they saw.[52] Similarly, to make a red heifer they would pass a red cup in front of the female cow as the male cow mounts her.[53] This worked with women as well, since they would pass in front of the handsome Rebbi Yochanan after they went to the mikve so that they would give birth to handsome children.[54] The important people of Rome knew of this method as well, as they would have relations in front of beautiful images on seals that they would look at, and after a time they would have beautiful Jewish children tied to their bed to look at in order to have beautiful offspring.[55]

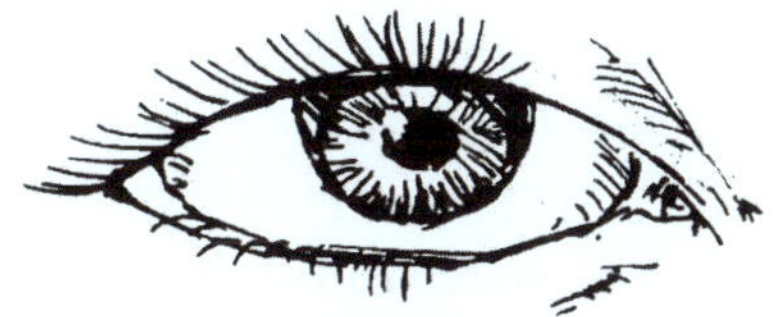 

52　Rashi Vayetzei 30:38.
53　Avodah Zarah 24a.
54　Berachos 20a.
55　Gittin 58a.

Things that Stretched

We know that there are materials such as rubber bands that can stretch. What is more amazing is when non-elastic material stretches miraculously. Here are a few examples: The Giant Og's teeth,[56] the arm of Pharoah's daughter Batya,[57] the poles of the Aron and wings of the Cherubim,[58] the tongues of the 10 bad spies,[59] the scepter of Achashverosh,[60] the stones that were erected in Gilgal,[61] and the metal tip of Pinchas' spear.[62]

---

56   Berachos 54b.
57   Sota 12b.
58   Yalkut Shimoni Teruma 367.
59   Sota 35a.
60   Megilla 15b.
61   Sifsei Cohen Ki Tavo.
62   Bamidbar Rabbah 20:25.

Inanimate Objects that Spoke

We all know that Hashem gave us the power of speech, and in fact Targum Onkelos on Breishis 2:4 states that man was created with the power of speech. What is interesting is that there are examples of inanimate beings speaking for an instant in time. These include: The lottery before entering Eretz Yisrael revealed which tribe was getting which parcel of land,[63] the staff of Moshe told what has happened with him,[64] the Sefer Hazichronos spoke up on behalf of Mordechai and what he had done,[65] in Beis Din the Judgement itself spoke at times,[66] the stones that David threw to Golias,[67] the stones that Yaakov slept on argued over who should have the privilege,[68] the boundary around Har Sinai at the giving of the Torah,[69] the Well of Miriam,[70] the Etz Hadaas Tov Vera told the snake not to touch him,[71] the Golden Calf said "I am the Lord your G-d," [72] the ground itself spoke during Korach's descent,[73] the Ten Commandments,[74] the different trees arguing over who should be the one to hang Haman,[75] and the different mountains over who should have the privilege of receiving the Torah.[76]

---

63   Bamidbar Rabbah 21:9.
64   Yalkut Shimoni 171.
65   Megilla 15b.
66   Megadim Chadashim Ekev in the name of Smuchim Laad.
67   Midrash Hagadol Ki Tetzei 21:10.
68   Chullin 91b.
69   Yalkut Meom Loez Yisro Miracle 24.
70   Rashi Chukas 21:17.
71   Yalkut Shimoni Breshis 25.
72   Tosfos Hashalem Ki Tisa 32:11,6; Ohr Hachaim Ki Tisa 32:19; Yalkut Reuveini Ki Tisa.
73   Tosfos Yom Tov Avot 5:6.
74   Shir Hashirim 1[2]:2.
75   Esther Rabbah 9:2.
76   Midrash Tehillim 68.

Plants that can't be Grafted

The Torah forbids grafting one tree to another.[77] There are certain plants though, that won't accept a graft even if one tries. These include: the grapevine,[78] the olive tree,[79] The date palm,[80] and grass.[81]

---

77 Kedoshim 19:9.
78 Zohar Vayera 115b.
79 Yerushalmi Kilayim 1:7.
80 Megadim Chadashim Ekev in the name of Ben Beisi.
81 Ahavas Olam from Rav Shlomo Algazi 119.

Upon Death the Worms do not Destroy the Body and the Bones don't Rot

We know normally upon death the body disintegrates, but there are miraculous exceptions to this when the body after death remains intact. For example, in the case of someone who always makes a blessing before and after he eats food,[82] or someone who is not jealous of others,[83] or someone who is holy in the way they eat, sleep, or have relations,[84] and on every Shabbos.[85] There are individuals themselves who have not experienced the rotting of the flesh after burial. For example, Avraham, Yitzchak, Yaakov, Moshe, Aharon, Miriam, Binyomin, [86] Shaul and Yehonatan,[87] and Rabbi Eliezer son of Rashbi.[88] The entire generation that heard the voice of Hashem at Har Sinai,[89] and someone who is buried in Eretz Yisrael also have no decomposition of the body.[90]

---

82   Sifsei Cohen Ekev.
83   Shabbos 152b.
84   Marganisa Dechasidei Bavel in the name of Reishis Chochma.
85   Baal Haturim Beshalach 16:24.
86   Baba Basra 17a.
87   Pirkei Derebbi Eliezer 17.
88   Ben Yehoyada Baba Metzia 84b.
89   Pirkei Derebbi Eliezer 41.
90   Megadim Chadashim Ekev in the name of Tov Yerushalayim.

People going without Sleep

We are told that we are supposed to get a good night's sleep and yet there are certain individuals who went without sleep for short or long periods of time. Noach, Shem, Cham, and Yafet did not "taste sleep" the entire year of the Mabul (Flood).[91] Yaakov didn't sleep the fourteen years he was learning in the yeshiva of Shem and Ever,[92] or during the twenty years he was at Lavan's house.[93] There was also a lack of sleep for Moshe during the forty day periods that he was on Har Sinai,[94] for Yehoshua after he met the angel,[95] for Bnei Yisrael during the Simchat Beis Hashoeva,[96] for Esther, Mordechai and Haman during that fateful night,[97] and for Elisha the whole time he was on the road.[98]

---

91 Tanchuma Noach 9.
92 Breishis Raba 68:11.
93 Breshis Raba 68:11.
94 Yalkut Shimoni Ki Tisa 406.
95 Megillah 3a.
96 Sukah 53a.
97 Yalkut Shimoni Esther 1957.
98 Chut Shel Chesed Vaera.

Unusual Length of Pregnancies

A standard pregnancy is generally nine months long. There have been instances of unusual length of pregnancies. For example, initially Chava got pregnant and gave birth within an hour.[99] During the time of the Mabul (Flood) a woman would get pregnant and deliver in one or three days, depending on which opinion is read.[100] Ovad's wife and eight daughters-in-law gave birth after seven days of pregnancy.[101] Another opinion states that it was every 14 days that Ovad's wife and eight daughter's-in-law would give birth.[102] In Mitzrayim, Bnei Yisrael would give birth when they wanted to within three months.[103] There was a woman who gave birth after 12 months of gestation,[104] Yisachar was delivered after 12 or 14 months of gestation,[105] and finally Rachel gave birth to Binyomin after eighteen months of gestation.[106]

---

99 Sanhedrin 38b.
100 Breishis Rabbah 36:1.
101 Yerushlami Yevamos 4:12.
102 Bamidbar Rabbah 4:20; Ben Yehoyada Brachos 63b.
103 Toldos Yitzchak (Kairo) 1:6.
104 Yevamos 80b.
105 Seder Hadoros.
106 Seder Hadoros.

Things that had many Tastes to them

We all know that the Manna in the Midbar could taste like anything one wanted.[107] What is not well known is that there were other things that also had many tastes to them. For example, the bird called Slav,[108] the Well of Miriam,[109] the food that Yaakov brought to Yitzchak,[110] and the Carob fruit that Rashbi and his son survived on in the cave.[111]

---

107 Mechilte Yisro Vayishma Yisro.
108 Baal Haturim Behaalosecha 11:20.
109 Midrash Talpiot Yayin.
110 Breshis Rabbah 67:2.
111 Sifsei Tzadik Lag Baomer 5.

Longevity after the Mabul (Flood)

There are many people recorded in the Torah who lived extraordinary long lives. However, the longevity of man decreased with time after the Mabul and although Moshe lived until 120, after that the lifespan of a man followed the sentence in Tehillim 90:10 that generally one lives to 70 but with strength 80 years are attainable. There are quite a few exceptions though and we will list some.

Og and Sichon lived more than 500 years.[112] Mordechai lived more than 400 years.[113] Zimri lived at least 250 years.[114] Pharoah of Avraham's time lived until Yechezkel (1000 years).[115] Yair and Machir sons of Menashe lived at least 219 years.[116] Iyov lived 210 years.[117] Chiram lived close to 1200 years or 600 years.[118] Pinchas lived more than 300 years.[119] Achiyah Hashiloni lived more than 500 years.[120] Micha lived more than 400 years.[121] Boaz (Ivtzan) lived more than 300 years,[122] or more than 400 years,[123] or almost 500 years.[124] Ovad lived more than 400 years,[125] or almost 500 years.[126] Efron lived at least 370 years.[127] Yocheved lived at least 210 years,[128] or at least 671 years.[129] Shem lived until King Solomon.[130] Yonatan ben Gershom lived almost 500 years.[131] Tzallephonis

---

112 Bamidbar Rabbah 19:32.
113 Seder Hadoros 3404.
114 Maharsha Sanhedrin 82b.
115 Rokeach Vayigash 47:8.
116 Baba Basra 121a.
117 Baba Basra 15a.
118 Breshis Rabbah 85:4.
119 Radak Shoftim 20:28.
120 Baba Basra 121b.
121 Seder Hadoros..
122 Rashi Divrei Hayamim 1,2:11.
123 Breishis Rabbah 96:4.
124 Midrash Hagadol Vayechi 47:29.
125 Breishis Rabbah 96:4.
126 Midrash Hagadol Vayechi 47:29.
127 If Efron is the Anak, Taama Dekra Chayei Sarah.
128 Sedr Olam Rabbah 9.
129 If Yocheved was the wise woman of Shmuel 2,20,16, Yalkut Meom Loez.
130 Megadim Chadashim in the name of Zichron Shmuel.
131 Yerushalmi Berachos 9b.

lived more than 370 years.[132] The 31 or 62 kings that Yehoshua killed lived more than 440 years.[133] Achiman, Sheishai and Talmi lived more than 1380 years.[134] Rav Preida lived more than 400 years.[135] Rav Yochanan lived 400 years.[136]

---

132 If Tzallephonis was the wife of On ben Pelles, Gilgul Neshamos.
133 Breishis Rabbah 53:10.
134 Tanna Debei Eliyahu 29; Yalkut Shimoni 742.
135 Eiruvin 54b.
136 Megadim Chadashim Berachos 48a in the name of Seder Tanaim Veamoraim.

The Language of the Birds

Whenever we hear birds chirping, although it might be pleasing to the ears, to the ordinary person it is nothing more than that. However, there were people who had the gift of hearing the sounds that birds make and interpreting those sounds as language. The following is a list of such people who had that ability:

Chava.[137]

Noach.[138]

Shlomo Hamelech.[139]

A man next to Rav Ilish.[140]

Rav Kahana.[141]

Hillel.[142]

Rabbi Yochanan ben Zakai.[143]

A Matron with Avuha Deshmuel.[144]

Rabbeinu Aharon Halevi from Barcelona.[145]

The Arizal.[146]

Habaal Shem Tov.[147]

---

137 Even Ezra Breshis 3:1.
138 Sanhedrin 108b.
139 Shir Hashirim Rabbah 1,[1], 9.
140 Gitin 45a.
141 Rabeinu Chananel Chulin 139b.
142 Sofrim 16:9.
143 Igeres Dekallah Vayigash.
144 Mesoras Hashas Kiddushin73a.
145 Meeras Aniyim from Rabbeinu Yitzchak of Akko.
146 Shaar Ruach Hakodesh 3.
147 Magid Devarav Leyaakov.

Old Women that Nursed

Mothers who nurse their babies are a common occurrence. It is not so common for an old woman to have the ability to give birth and to have the ability to nurse her baby.

These women miraculously nursed babies:

Sarah.[148]

Yocheved.[149]

Naomi.[150]

---

148 Vayera 21:7.
149 Sotah 12b.
150 Alshich Ruth 4:16.

Old Women who Gave Birth

Generally, through the natural order of things there is a certain age after which women can no longer give birth. These women miraculously give birth much later in life:

Sarah at age 90.[151]

Yocheved at age 130.[152]

Chana at age 130.[153]

---

151 Lech Lecha 17:17.
152 Pirkei Derebbi Eliezer 48.
153 Midrash Talpiot Chana.

How many Children can one Man have?

We hear of an average family having an average number of children. Some families have more than the average. And although we don't know how many wives some of these people had, the number of children they had can only be described as miraculous.

Izevel and Achav had 140 children.[154]

Gideon had 70 children.[155]

Avdon ben Hillel had 40 sons.[156]

Haman had 208 sons.[157]

Boaz (Ivtzan) had 30 sons and 30 daughters.[158]

Kayin had 100 children.[159]

Yair Hagiladi had 30 sons.[160]

Iyov had altogether 21 sons and 6 daughters.[161]

Rechavam had 28 sons and 60 daughters.[162]

Avihu had 22 sons and 16 daughters.[163]

King David had 400 sons,[164] or 600 sons.[165]

A Yibum that performed a Levirate Marriage with 12 women had 36 children in 3 years.[166]

---

154 Yalkut Shimoni Melachim 232.

155 Shoftim 8:30.

156 Shoftim 12:14.

157 Megillah 15b.

158 Baba Basra 91a.

159 Shmos Rabbah 31:17.

160 Shoftim 10:4.

161 Iyov.1:2, Rashi Iyov 42:13.

162 Divrei Hayamim 2,11:21.

163 Divrei Hayamim 2, 13:21.

164 Kidushin 76b, Megadim Chadashim Ki Teztei in the name of Yad Rama on Sanhedrin.

165 Yalkut Meor Haafela Ki Tetzei.

166 Yerushalmi Yevamos 4:12.

Fasting for forty Days

There is a limit to how long someone can fast and still be alive. Forty days of fasting is well beyond that limit, and only through a miracle do these examples exist.

Moshe on Har Sinai.[167]

Bnei Yisrael during the last set of forty days Moshe was on Har Sinai.[168]

Shlomo Hamelech.[169]

Eliyahu.[170]

The sheep of Yisro that Moshe was shepherding.[171]

---

167 Ekev 9:9.
168 Tana Debei Eliyahu Zuta 4.
169 Yalkut Shimoni Mishlei 929.
170 Melachim 1, 19:8.
171 Midrash Hagadol Shmos 3:1; Midrash Agada Shmos 3:1.

Sextuplets

In today's world with fertility treatments, multiple births happen more commonly than before fertility treatments were available. Nonetheless there have been sextuplets that have occurred before the era of modern medicine. These time periods produced sextuplets:

The Bnei Elohim took the daughters of man.[172]

The generation of the Dispersion (Haflaga).[173]

Bnei Yisroel in Mitzrayim.[174]

The wife and eight daughters-in-law of Oved Adam.[175]

---

172 Midrash Hagadol Breishis 6:4; Pirkei Derebbi Eliezer 22.
173 Pirkei Derebbi Eliezer 24.
174 Shmos Rabbah 1:8.
175 Shmuel 2, 6:10; Berachos 63b.

The Earth Swallows up items

We are familiar with earthquakes that wreak havoc on large areas. There are several instances though in the Torah, where the earth swallowed up things, but it was not an earthquake. In an earthquake the earth opens, but in these instances not only did the earth open up, but it closed up afterwards, leaving no trace.

The Blood of Hevel.[176]

Hevel himself.[177]

At the time Lemech killed Kayim, the earth swallowed up four families of Kayim: Chanoch, Irad, Mechuyel and Mesushael.[178]

The Mitzrim at Yam Suf.[179]

Korach.[180]

The people of Nineveh after repenting went back to their evil ways and the dead were swallowed up into the ground below.[181]

The babies in Mitzrayim were swallowed up into the ground.[182]

A third of the Tower of Bavel was swallowed into the ground.[183]

The Beis Hamikdash was not destroyed but instead swallowed up in its place.[184]

The gates of the Beis Hamikdash.[185]

Pithom.[186]

---

176 Breshis 4:11.

177 Ohr Hachaim Breshis 4:14.

178 Midrash Hagadol Breishis 4:23; Tanchuma Breishis 11.

179 Beshalach 15:12.

180 Korach 16:32.

181 Yalkut Shimoni Yona 550.

182 Sotah 11b.

183 Sefer Hayashar Noach.

184 Midbar Kadmos 40:43.

185 Eicha Rabbah 2:13.

186 Sotah 11a.

Immobile People

There can be medical conditions that render a person unable to move. There are amazing situations where people have been miraculously stopped in their tracks and unable to move. Here are some famous cases:

The Mitzrim during the last three days of the Plague of Darkness.[187]

Pharoah.[188]

Golias.[189]

Anyone that the Aron captured for Death.[190]

Rebbi Liezer, Rebbi Yehoshua, and Rebbi Akiva.[191]

A heretic at Shaar Dimusin.[192]

---

187 Shmos Rabbah 14:3.
188 Shmos Rabbah 9:2.
189 Vayikra Rabbah 21:2.
190 Benayahu Yevamos 79a.
191 Yerushalmi Sanhedrin 7:13.
192 Yerushalmi Sanhedrin 7:13.

Animals that Spoke with People

Any child of the 60's can relate to the talking horse Mr. Ed, or the talking mule Francis. What is remarkable is that there have been many instances where Hashem has animals speaking with people as if it is the most normal thing. Here are a few examples:

The Snake in Gan Eden.[193]

The Donkey with Bilam.[194]

The Cows of the Plishtim sang a song of praise as they returned the Aron.[195]

The Chol bird (Orishena), the Raven and the Dove all spoke with Noach.[196]

A scorpion spoke with Rav Yochanan,[197] a frog spoke with King David,[198] a wolf spoke with Yaakov,[199] Eliyahu's cow spoke with Eliyahu,[200] a chicken spoke with King Shlomo,[201] frogs from the Plague spoke with the Mitzrim,[202] and the fish spoke with Yonah.[203]

Every horse at Kriyas Yam Suf replied to their Mitzri rider.[204]

And like the famous Dr. Doolittle, the following people spoke with many different animals: Adam,[205] Chava,[206] Noach,[207] and King Shlomo.[208]

---

193 Breishis 3:1.
194 Balak 22:28.
195 Avodah Zara 24a.
196 Sanhedrin 108a.
197 Torah Shleima Breshis 2 from Hamaaseyos.
198 Zohar Pinchas 232a.
199 Meom Loez Vayeshev.
200 Bamidbar Rabbah 23:9.
201 Targum Sheini Esther 1:3.
202 Shmos Rabbah 15:27.
203 Meom Loez Yonah 2:2.
204 Shmos Rabbah 23:14.
205 Breshis Rabbah 20:8.
206 Even Ezra Breshis 3:1.
207 Etz Yosef Tanchuma Noach 12.
208 Meom Loez Malachim 1, 5:13.

Waters Split

We all know of the amazing miracle where the waters of the Yam Suf split and allowed Bnei Yisrael to walk through on dry land. This miracle repeated itself in other avenues several times.

Moshe and Bnei Yisrael through the Yam Suf.[209]

Dasan and Avirum through the Yam Suf.[210]

Yaakov and the Yarden.[211]

Yehoshua and Bnei Yisrael and the Yarden.[212]

The mighty warriors who helped King David and the Yarden.[213]

A heretic near Rebbi Yehoshua by water.[214]

Rebbi Pinchas ben Yair and the river Genai three times.[215]

Eliyahu and water.[216]

Elisha and water.[217]

Rebbbi Chanina and the waters of Tiveria.[218]

A Chasid and water.[219]

---

209 Beshalach 14.
210 Beer Mayim Chaim Beshalach.
211 Tanchuma Yashan Vayetzei 3.
212 Yehoshua 3:16.
213 Divrei Hayamim 1, 12:16.
214 Yerushalmi Sanhedrin 7:13.
215 Chulin 7a.
216 Melachim 2, 2:8.
217 Melachim 2, 2:14.
218 Yerushalmi Avodah Zara 3:1.
219 Psikta Derebbi Kahana 18:5.

Animals that Nursed Humans

There is a modern tale by Rudyard Kipling called the Jungle Book, about a boy raised by wolves in the Jungle. We have in our Midrashic works a much earlier scenario.

A wolf nursed Romos and Romilus.[220]

A dog nursed Koresh.[221]

---

220 Esther Rabbah 3:8, Midrash Tehillim 17.
221 Mayane Yeshoua 8:3.

Giants

There have been many recorded giants in modern day record books, but none the sizes of the amazing giants that are in the Torah world. Here are some with their sizes:

Adam was reduced in size to 100 amos tall.[222]

Og was as tall as six people,[223] or his feet were 18 amos long,[224] or his height until his ankle was 30 amos,[225] or his thigh bone was 3 parsaos,[226] and his crib was 9 amos by 4 amos.[227]

Before the Mabul (Flood), people were 100 amos tall.[228] The Nephilim (fallen angels) were 100 amos tall.[229] Avraham was as tall as 74 people,[230] and Yitzchak was as tall as Avraham.[231] Tamar was as tall as a Date tree.[232]

Moshe was 10 amos tall,[233] and grew after the plague of darkness.[234] Some say all of the Leviim were 10 amos tall,[235] others say only Bnei Kahas were 10 amos tall,[236] still others say the Leviim other than Moshe were 7 amos tall,[237] finally some say some Leviim were 5 amos tall.[238] Finally, there is an opinion that everyone in the generation of the Midbar was 10 amos tall.[239]

During the time of the spies, the giants that lived in Eretz Yisrael

---

222 Breishis Rabbah 12:6; Baba Basra 75a.
223 Taame Dekra Lech Lecha.
224 Devarim Rabbah 1:24.
225 Berachos 54a.
226 Nidah 24b.
227 Devarim 3:11.
228 Baal Haturim Noach 6:13.
229 Rabeinu Ephraim Breishis.
230 Sofrim 21:9.
231 Baba Metzia 87a.
232 Rabeinu Ephraim Vayeshev.
233 Berachos 54b.
234 Maharzav on Shmos Rabbah 18:1.
235 Shabbas 92a.
236 Haramaz Haeyur on Meiri Shabbos 92a.
237 Ritva on Shabbos 92a.
238 Panim Yafos Teruma.
239 Megadim Chadashim Beshalach in the name of Meir Aynai Chachamim.

were 60 amos tall,[240] whereas the regular people there were as tall as Golias (6 amos and a zeres).[241] All of the spies were also 60 amos tall.[242] Another opinion states Yehoshua was 5 amos tall.[243] Golias was 6 amos and a zeres tall.[244] King Shaul was taller than everyone.[245] And David became 6 amos tall.[246] The Mitzri that Benayahu ben Yehoyada killed was 5 amos tall.[247]

---

240 Midrash Pisaron Torah Shelach.
241 Midrash Agada Shelach.
242 Hadar Zekainim Shelach.
243 Otzar Midrashim 210; Midrash Talpiot Yehoshua.
244 Shmuel 1, 17:4.
245 Shmuel 1, 9:2.
246 Meom Loez Shmuel 1, 17:51.
247 Divrei Hayamim 1, 11:23.

When the Sun Stood Still

We really don't have a modern-day equivalent for the sun standing still. It's clearly not an eclipse. Did the earth suddenly stop rotating on its axis? The exact mechanism may not be known, but we do have a record of when the phenomena happened.

For Kayin.[248]

For Yaakov.[249]

The year of the Mabul (Flood).[250]

The day of leaving Mitzrayim, the splitting of the sea, the war with Amalek, the receiving of the Torah, and the event at Nachalei Arnon.[251]

At Matan Torah the sun stood still for three days![252]

At the wars with Og and Sichon.[253]

For Moshe when he said, "Listen Sky…."[254]

For Yehoshua.[255]

For Moshe, Yehoshua and Nekedimon ben Gurion.[256]

In the time of Korach.[257]

For King David.[258]

For King Chizkiyahu.[259]

For Eliyahu.[260]

For Aba Tachana Chasida.[261]

---

248 Breishis Rabbah 22:12.
249 Chulin 91b.
250 Sifsei Chachamim Noach 8:22.
251 Rabeinu Bechai Yisro.
252 Megadim Chadashim Yisro.
253 Rashi Devarim 2:25; Rashi Avodah Zara 25a.
254 Sifre Haazeinu.
255 Yehoshua 10:12.
256 Taanis 20a.
257 Nedarim 39b.
258 Shmuel 2, 5:20; Midrash Hagadol Devraim 2:25.
259 Yeshayahu 38:8.
260 Psikte Rabasi 4 on Melachim 1, 18:36.
261 Koheles Rabbah 9:7.

Only Boys were Born

Today, there are expensive medical means to guarantee the sex of your child. There are many Segulos also available to increase the chances of having a male child. However, there have been certain times in history that miraculously only boys were born:

In Mitzrayim, they all delivered boys.[262]

In Mitzrayim, they delivered six boys at a time.[263]

Right after Matan Torah, anyone whose wife got pregnant had a boy.[264]

During the time of Korach, when Moshe was wrongly suspected of infidelity.[265]

During the Midbar, Naftali's tribe only gave birth to boys.[266]

Right after the inauguration of the Beis Hamikdash, anyone whose wife got pregnant had a boy.[267]

The wife and daughters-in-law of Oved Adam gave birth to male sextuplets.[268]

In Kfar Dichrin.[269]

When the Halacha was like Rebbi Elazar son of Rebbi Shimon, all were blessed to have boys.[270]

---

262 Panim Yafos Shmos.

263 Beis Elokim 21.

264 Rashi Shabbos 89b.

265 Peer Mikdashim Pinchas in the name of Sifsei Chachamim Satmar.

266 Lekach Tov Bamidbar.

267 Moed Katan 9.

268 Shmuel 2 6:10, Petach Anayim Shabbos 30b.

269 Eichah Rabbah 2:4.

270 Baba Metzia 84b.

A Sin Detector

We know that police often use a machine called a lie detector that measures responses to various questions to find out if a person is telling the truth or not. While not allowed in court rooms, such devices have been invaluable to force confessions to get to the truth. There is no modern machine that can tell if a person has committed a sin. Yet long ago there were many instances where the truth would miraculously be discovered.

Noach's ark would not allow animals in that did not keep to their own kind.[271] The tree of Avraham would not provide shade for idol worshippers.[272] The heavenly cloud in the Midbar would expel the tribe of Dan who worshipped idols,[273] whoever needed a Mikve,[274] and because of one's sins.[275] The Manna fell on the doorsteps of the righteous, but the sinners had to go far to gather it. Depending on where the Manna would fall, would also elucidate in a married couple who sinned against who.[276]

From the Midianites, whoever sinned the sun would shine directly on him, [277] and they would be passed in front of the Tzitz to know who was ready for relations, as were the inhabitants of Gilad were be placed on a wine barrel for the same reason.[278] The descendants of Shaul were passed in front of the Aron to determine who would die.[279]

Every tribe who did a sin, their stone on the Choshen would darken.[280] And with the story with Achan, the Aron and the Choshen together identified the sinner.[281] The Aron could also differentiate be-

---

271 Zevachim 116a.
272 Zohar Vayera 102b.
273 Tanchuma Ki Tetzei 10.
274 Pirke Derebbi Eliezer 44.
275 Rashi Ki Teztei 25:18.
276 Yoma 75a.
277 Tanchuma Balak 19.
278 Yevamos 60b.
279 Yevamos 79a.
280 Tanchuma Vayeshev 2.
281 Rashi and Radak Yehoshua 7: 14-17.

tween the circumcised and non-circumcised.[282]

Worms from the Egla Arufah would travel to the murderer's house.[283] Worms also left the home of Dasan and Avirom who left over the Manna.[284] A Rasha who would bring a Korban not designated for his sin would have the smoke go up crookedly.[285] Drinking the ground up golden calf in water would test the sinner,[286] just like the Sotah woman.[287] And whoever kissed the golden calf whole heartedly would be identifiable by having golden lips.[288]

The letters of the Tzitz would only shine on the face on those who didn't sin.[289] Bnei Yisrael[290] and their wives[291] were tested by water at Mei Meriva (Bitter Waters).

282 Yalkut Shimoni Divrei Hayamim 2, 1085.
283 Targum Yonatan ben Uzeil Shoftim 21:8.
284 Tanchuma Vayeztei 11.
285 Yalkut Reuveni Vayikra.
286 Targum Yonatan ben Uziel Ki Tisa 32:20.
287 Naso 5:24.
288 Pirkei Derebbi Eliezer 45.
289 Zohar Vayakel 217b.
290 Mayan Beis Hashoeva Chukas.
291 Zohar Naso 124b.

Waters Rising

There is no natural explanation for water rising as an individual approaches and yet this has happened miraculously for certain individuals over time.

For the sheep of Avraham.[292]

For people who needed at Mikve at the spring under Avraham's tree.[293]

For Bnei Yisrael and Beer Miriam.[294]

For Rivka at the well.[295]

For Yaakov at the well with Rachel.[296]

For Yaakov when he came to the Nile.[297]

For Moshe watering the sheep of Yisro.[298]

---

292 Breishis Rabbah 54:5.

293 Zohar Vayera 102b.

294 Breishis Rabbah 54:5.

295 Breshis Rabbah 60:5.

296 Targum Yonatan ben Uziel 29:10.

297 Kli Yakar Vayigash 47:8.

298 Zohar Vayetzei 152a.

Things that can Carry Themselves and Other Things

There are certain items that float in the air and do not need to be held to move around. This is truly miraculous and cannot be replicated in nature. There are also certain items that not only could transport themselves but had the ability to transport others in proximity. Here is a list of such items that had each property.

Transport itself:

The first Luchos.[299]

All the utensils of the Mishkan.[300]

The task of Bnei Kahat that "carried" the Aron and other utensils, and the task of Bnei Gershon that "carried" the curtains, Ohel Moed and its covering.[301]

The Aron of the Luchos.[302]

The Aron of wood that Moshe made.[303]

The Aron of Yosef.[304]

The staff of Moshe.[305]

The stones of the Beis Hamikdash.[306]

Everything that can transport other things can of course transport itself.[307]

Transport other things too:

The Aron.[308]

---

299 Ohr Hachaim Ekev 10:1.

300 Tzror Hamor Naso.

301 Megadim Chadashim in the name of Deveres Shalom.

302 Bamidbar Rabbah 4:20.

303 Shach Teruma.

304 Tosfos Hashalem Veyechi; Moshav Zekainim Vayechi.

305 Sechel Tov Shemos 4:20.

306 Shir Hashirim Rabbah 1:5.

307 Sotah 35.

308 Sotah 35.

The utensils that Bnei Kahat "carried".[309]

At the time the Urim and Tumim were in the Choshen.[310]

The wagons that "carried" the Mishkan.[311]

---

309 Megadim Chadashim Bamidbar in the name of Hachafetz Chaim Naso.
310 Meshech Chochma Titzave 28:30.
311 Ohr Haganuz Naso.

Sheidim (Demons)

The Talmud tells us some basics about Sheidim. In three ways they are like angels: they have wings, can fly from one end of the world to the other and know the future; and in three ways they are like people: they can eat and drink, multiply and die.[312] But there are many other properties that Sheidim have. For example, there are Jewish Sheidim and non-Jewish Sheidim.[313] Sheidim can transform themselves into different appearances / animals.[314] Male Sheidim have hair only on their head,[315] or have hair on their head, whereas female Sheidim do not.[316] They have been described as evil spirits.[317]

A most fascinating thing is that a person can separate their "good part" from their "bad part or Sheid" during their lifetime.[318] A female Sheid can mate with a human male, and then changes her outer appearance to a male Sheid, who then impregnates a human female.[319] And in fact, there have been people who have sent their Sheid instead of themselves on occasion:

Yosef with the wife of Potiphar.[320]

Sarah with Pharoah.[321]

Esther with Achashverosh.[322]

Yael with Sisra.[323]

---

312 Chagiga 16a.

313 Zohar Pinchas 253a, Ben Yehoyada Gitin 68b.

314 Benayahu Gittin 68a, Tiferes Tzvi on the Zohar Breishis 54b.

315 Otzar Haplaos from Rayach Nichoach 10.

316 Tiferes Tzvi Zohar Breishis 54b.

317 Rashi Rosh Hashannah 28a.

318 Midrash Talpiot Achashverosh; Zohar Hachadash 41b.

319 Tiferes Tzvi Zohar Breishis 54b.

320 Sifsei Cohen Vayeshev; Zohar Ki Tetzei 276a.

321 Sifsei Cohen Vayeshev.

322 Sifsei Cohen Vayeshev; Zohar Ki Tetzei 276a.

323 Midbar Kadmos Yael.

Traveling on the Wings of Eagles

Hashem promised to bring us to him on the wings of eagles[324] and there were several times in the past that we traveled that way.

Bnei Yisrael to Ramses.[325]

Bnei Yisrael from Ramses to Eretz Yisrael to do the Korban Pesach.[326]

Bnei Yisrael from Ramses to Sukkos.[327]

Bnei Yisrael at Matan Torah when they went backwards from fright and then were brought forward.[328]

324　Yisro 19:4.

325　Mechilta Derebi Yishmael Yisro 2, Midrash Agadah Yisro 19.

326　Targum Yonatan ben Uziel Yisro 19:4.

327　Mechilte Derebi Yishmael Bo 14.

328　Mechilta Derebi Yishmael Yisro 2; Midrash Agadah Yisro 19.

Unusual Domesticated Animals' Behavior

Domesticated animals are tame and not aggressive. There have been amazing instances in the past when that was not so. Goats killed wolves.[329]

Goats carried bears in their horns.[330]

Moshe's sheep lay down upon wolves.[331]

Chickens tore up cats.[332]

Sheep were biting things in Yehudah.[333]

---

329 Baba Basra 15b.
330 Taanis 25a.
331 Yalkut Midrash Teiman Shmos 3:1.
332 Yerushalmi Peah 3:7.
333 Midrash Hagadol Haazeinu 32:24.

Things Swallowed up by Other Things

There were other miraculous events over time where things were swallowed up into other things aside from being swallowed into the ground.[334] The staffs of the magicians in Mitzrayim were swallowed up by Aharon's staff.[335] The magicians themselves were swallowed up by the staff of Aharon.[336] Moshe was swallowed by the Angel/Snake.[337] The staff of Aharon swallowed up the other tribes' staffs.[338] Yonah was swallowed by a fish.[339] The Manna was swallowed up in the limbs of the people,[340] as was any food of the merchants eaten at the same time,[341] as was the meat of the korbonos eaten then,[342] as was the water of the well of Miriam,[343] as was the Slav.[344] The shards of earthenware, the crop and feathers of the birds, the ashes of the inner Mizbeach and Menorah were all swallowed up in their place.[345] Blood was swallowed in the Paroches.[346] And the staff of Moshe which was previously planted in Yisro's garden, swallowed up anyone who approached it.[347]

---

334 Sefer Hayashar Noach.

335 Vaera 7:12.

336 Malbim Vaera 7:12.

337 Nedarim 31b.

338 Baal Haturim Vaera 7:12.

339 Yonah 2:1.

340 Yoma 75b.

341 Yuma 75b.

342 Ruach Chaim Avos 3:3.

343 Kli Yakar Chukas 21:5.

344 Ketzepichas Bedvash in the name of Aruch Laner on Sukkah 43b.

345 Yoma 21a.

346 Torah Ohr by the Shla on Taanis 54a.

347 Midrash Vayosha on Azi Vezimras Ya.

Transparent Things

We are all aware of transparent things in our daily life, such as glass, clear plastic or water. How miraculous it was to have other transparent objects in ancient times such as:

Har Sinai.[348]

The Lintel of the door in Mitzrayim.[349]

The Manna during the week except for Shabbos.[350]

The Tzintzenes (container) that kept the Manna for the future.[351]

The Aron of Yosef.[352]

The pathways within Kriyas Yam Suf.[353]

---

348 Targum Yonatan ben Uziel Yisro 19:17.
349 Maharil Diskin Bo.
350 Malbim Beshalach 31.
351 Abarbanel Beshalach 16.
352 Chupas Eliyahu 22.
353 Radal on Pirkei Derebbi Eliezer 42.

Pregnant Women who didn't Appear Pregnant

Generally, women begin to show their pregnancy in the second trimester. Some women don't show until even later than that. These women didn't appear pregnant at all:

Zilpa.[354]

Yocheved.[355]

Tziporah.[356]

---

354 Breshis Rabbah 71:9.
355 Revid Hazahav; Iyun Haparsha.
356 Lekach Tov 2:22.

People with Wings

For many generations man has dreamed to flying. The Wright brothers made their dream come true and today we have modern aviation. There were people in history who had their own set of wings to fly:

Shemaver.[357]

Mamre.[358]

Yochani.[359]

---

357 Rashi Lech Lecha 14:2.
358 Yalkut Shimoni Beshalach 235.
359 Yalkut Shimoni Beshalach 235.

Bestiality

It is hard to believe that people have been interested in such behavior, but we have incidences of this in history:

Adam.[360]

Bilam.[361]

Daryavesh.[362]

---

360 Yevamos 63a.
361 Avodah Zara 4b.
362 Rosh Hashannah 4a.

Premature Aging

There are unusual people whose hair turns white prematurely. Usually, we say that is due to their genes. However there have been people who have had old age suddenly occur:

Avraham.[363]

Yehoshua.[364]

Eli the Cohen.[365]

Shmuel.[366]

King David.[367]

King Shlomo.[368]

Barzilai Hagiladi.[369]

Rav Elazar ben Azariah.[370]

The Cohen Gadol.[371]

---

363 Tanchuma Shmini 3.
364 Tanchuma Chayei Sarah 2.
365 Tanchuma Chayei Sarah 2.
366 Taanis 5b.
367 Tanchuma Chayei Sarah 2.
368 Tanchuma Chayei Sarah 2.
369 Rashi Yevamos 76a.
370 Berachos 12b.
371 Magid Yosef from Toras Cohanim Emor.

Clothes that Grew or Shrunk

As kids grow, their clothes size grows too. As adults if we gain weight or lose weight we may have to enlarge or reduce our pants size or may even buy a new pair that fits. There were circumstances where a person changed size and the clothes that he/ she was wearing miraculously changed size as well.

When Moshe mentioned to Aharon he was going to die, his stature shortened as did the clothes he was wearing so they would fit his son Eliezer.[372]

The clothes of Shaul decreased in size when the future King David put them on.[373]

The clothes of the new Cohen Gadol adjusted themselves according to his size.[374]

The clothes received at Har Sinai from the angels grew with them as the people grew.[375]

The clothes of Asav that Yaakov put on during the blessings decreased in size to fit him.[376]

The cloak of Shmuel grew with him as he grew.[377]

---

372 Nachlas Yaakov Yehoshua.
373 Rashi Shmuel 1, 17:38; Nachlas Yaakov Yehoshua.
374 Tiferes Yonatan Titzave.
375 Shir Hashirim Rabbah 4:11.
376 Sifsei Cohen Toldos.
377 Yalkut Shimoni Shmuel 139.

Letters that Protrude or Light up

There were several objects in the past that had Hebrew letters on them and miraculously the letters either protruded or lit up to give a message for the reader. The most famous such object was of course the Urim Vetumim inside the Choshen.[378] The two Shoham Stones on the Ephod also had their letters give messages.[379] The last of the Cohen's garments that had letters on them was the Tzitz and it too gave messages.[380] Interesting there is also an opinion that the staff of Moshe also had its letters give messages,[381] as the letters of the plague would protrude as the plague was taking place. And whether we are speaking about the letters on the Choshen or the letters that were written on the Mashkof in Mitzrayim as the Angel of Death passed by, the Maharil Diskin states that they were written backwards, so when they let out light in front of them the could be read properly![382] He is consistent and says the same thing about the letters written on the large stones as Bnei Yisrael crossed over into Eretz Yisrael. They too were written backwards on the stones so that when limestone was attached, the limestone could be read in the proper order.[383]

---

378 Yuma 73b.
379 Tosfos Hashalem Tetzave 28:10.
380 Zohar Tetzave 218b.
381 Maharil Diskin Bo.
382 Maharil Diskin Bo, Titzave.
383 Chidushei Maharal Diskin Ki Tavo.

Stones that gave Sustenance

There were several times in history where Hashem created two stones to sustain babies. One stone would produce honey and the other milk or meal for the babies to nurse from:

The first instance we know of is with Avraham. After he was born, Terach hid him in a cave away from Nimrod, who wanted to kill him, and there he was sustained.[384] During the servitude in Mitzrayim, the women would give birth and leave the babies in the field to be sustained.[385] And all of the babies the Mitzrim threw into the Nile didn't die, but instead the river spit them out into the Midbar where they were sustained.[386]

384 Tzena Urena Lech Lecha.
385 Sefer Hayahar Shmos.
386 Yalkut Shimoni Shmos 165.

Indestructible by Fire

There are many materials that are labeled nonflammable, or fire resistant. These materials were engulfed in flames and yet did not burn:

The Burning Bush.[387]

The wood on the Mizbeach for sacrifices.[388]

The wood on the Mizbeach of gold.[389]

Har Sinai at Matan Torah.[390]

---

387 Shmos 3:2.
388 Vayikra Rabbah 7:5.
389 Vayikra Rabbah 7:5.
390 Shach Devarim 4:9.

Progeny at a Young Age

There are societal norms for the general age to marry and start a family. However, in the past, there were exceptions to the "normal" age to have a baby:

Haran fathered a baby at age six.[391]

Dina was six or seven when she gave birth to Asnas.[392]

Peretz was seven when he fathered Chetzron and eight when he fathered Chamol.[393]

Uri and his father Chur and his father Calev were all eight when they fathered children.[394]

Eliam and his father Achitophel were both eight or nine when they fathered children.[395]

Bat Sheva was six or seven when she gave birth.[396]

---

391 Breshis Rabbah 38:14.
392 Sofrim 21:9.
393 Daas Zkeinim Mebaalei Tosfos Vayeshev 38:1.
394 Sanhedrin 69b.
395 Sanhedrin 69b.
396 Sanhedrin 69b.

The Scent of Gan Eden

How we all strive to learn Torah and do Mitzvot so we can enter Gan Eden one day. And yet in the past there were times that the smell of Gan Eden was present in this world as a tease of the future.

When Yaakov went to get the blessings from Yitzchak.[397]

With Korban Pesach in Mitzrayim.[398]

With the bones of Yosef.[399]

With the Manna.[400]

In the smoke of Har Sinai.[401]

With the bedsheets of Elisha.[402]

In the whole house of Rashbi when Rebbi Shimon was gone.[403]

In the sukkah of Rav Mordechai Twersky (Rachmastoroyka).[404]

---

397 Tanchuma Toldos 11.
398 Shmos Rabbah 19:5.
399 Tzror Hamor Beshalach.
400 Zohar Beshalach 63a.
401 Zohar Yisro 84a.
402 Chomas Anach Melachim 2,
403 Zohar Haazeinu 296b.
404 Rav Shmuel Salant.

Unusual Pregnancies

There have been rare instances of unusual pregnancies. Super fecundation is a term used to indicate when a woman gets pregnant again after already carrying a pregnancy. Also sometimes with twins one twin gets delivered weeks after the first twin is delivered.

Gad and Asher perhaps were twins, Gad born after seven months, and Asher after nine.[405]

Yehuda and Chizkiyahu were twins, one born after seven months and one after nine.[406]

Onan and Shelah were twins. While Bat Shua was pregnant with Onan, she got pregnant again with Shelah.[407]

---

405 Meshech Chochma Vayetzei.
406 Yevamos 65b.
407 Tosfos Hashalem Vayeshev.

Transformation into Animals

There are many instances of people turning themselves into animals or being turned into animals. This is different than being reincarnated into an animal as a gilgul for a punishment of a sin done in this world. Here are some cases of people that became animals:

In the generation of the Mabul (Flood), some were punished and became monkeys and elephants.[408]

In the generation of the Haflaga (Dispersion), some were punished and became monkeys[409] or elephants,[410] whereas others were turned into bears.[411]

Nebuchadneztar was turned into a female animal that grazed grass.[412]

Serach Bas Asher was turned into a doe and warned a tyrant to be good to the Jews.[413]

Binyamin could turn himself into a wolf.[414]

Pharoah's magicians turned themselves into snakes.[415]

The Amalekim could turn themselves into animals.[416]

Agag turned himself into a fat cow and turned his wife into one to get her pregnant before he got killed.[417]

---

408 Maleches Shlomo Kilayim 8:6.
409 Sanhedrin 109a.
410 Sefer Hayashar Noach.
411 Siddur Harokeach 172.
412 Daniel 4:33; Rashi Shabbos 150a.
413 Maaseh Gedolim Pinchas 23.
414 Rabeinu Ephraim Breishis, Vayechi.
415 Eretz Chemda Vaera.
416 Baal Haturim Mishpatim 22:17; Rashi Shmuel 1. 15:3.
417 Moshav Zekeinim Beshalach 17:8.

Rabbi Pinchas ben Yair's Donkey

Rabbi Pinchas ben Yair was a very holy man. And so, it is only fitting that his donkey would reflect the holiness of his owner. There are many stories associated with that donkey and here are a few:

That donkey refused to eat from untithed produce.[418]

The donkey was punished because he brought the Rabbi to an unclean place while the Rabbi was thinking thoughts of Torah.[419]

The donkey on one occasion saved Jews from robbers.[420]

The donkey didn't want to proceed when he smelled the scent of Rashbi approaching.[421]

---

418 Chulin 7a.
419 Nefesh Chaim 47.
420 Zohar Balak 200b.
421 Zohar Pinchas 221b.

Seeing Sound

We have five senses, and under normal conditions we hear sounds and see pictures. Miraculously, in the past there were circumstances where people saw sounds! The most famous one is of course seeing the sounds of the ten commandments, but there are others.

Adam before the sin.[422]

Avraham when Hashem spoke with him.[423]

The brothers of Yosef when he revealed himself to them.[424]

Bnei Yisrael at Har Sinai.[425]

Shmuel the Seer.[426]

---

422 Tiferes Shlomo Parshas Hachodesh.
423 Afsei Eretz Lech Lecha.
424 Divrei Yoel Vayigash.
425 Mechilte Yisro.
426 Yitav Lecha Lech Lecha.

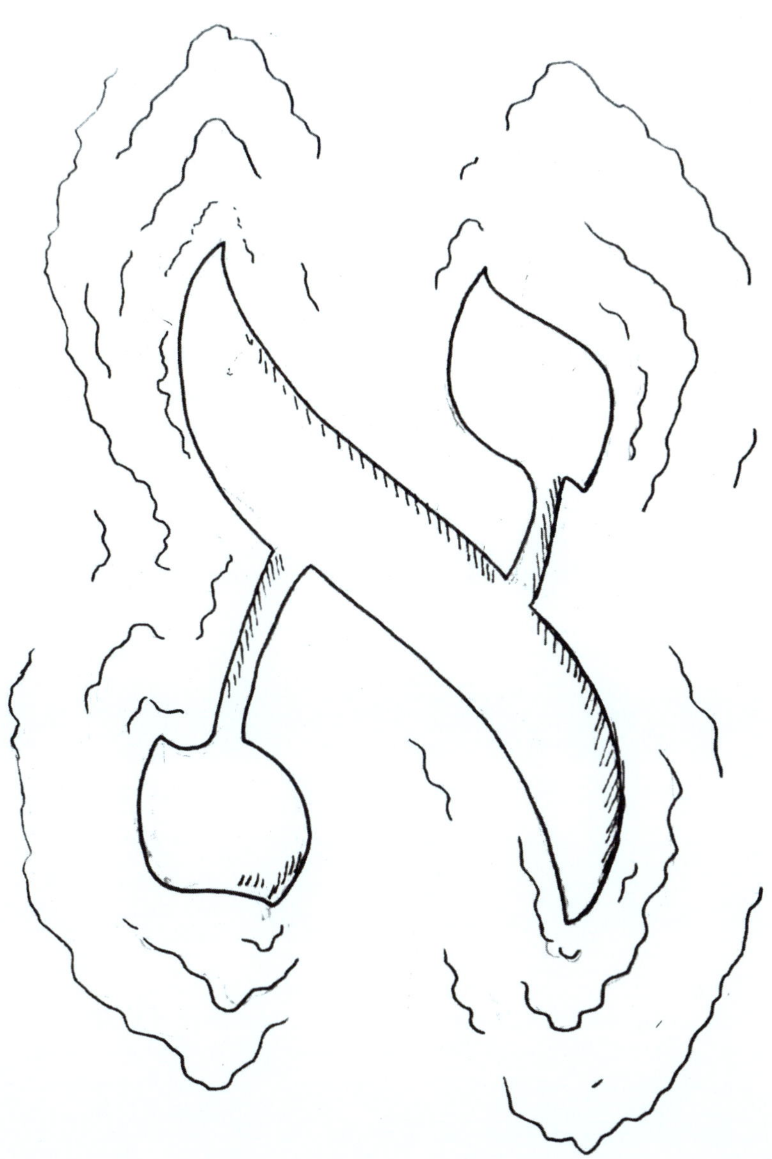

The Lintel is Raised

There have been a few times where for various reasons a doorway was not big enough to pass through and it miraculously was raised to avoid a problem.

Avraham visiting Avimelech would have had to bow down to an idol placed on a low doorway, but since the lintel was raised, he avoided that.[427]

Yaakov was visiting Pharoah, and he too would have had to bow down to an idol place over a low doorway, but since the lintel was raised, he avoided that.[428]

When Pinchas carried Zimri and Cosbi on his spear, the Lintel miraculously was raised so could walk out of the tent with them held high.[429]

---

427 Tsena Urene Vayigash.
428 Tsena Urena Vayigash.
429 Sanhedrin 82b.

Necks became Marble

There were several instances of a neck miraculously turning to marble, to save someone from being harmed.

Yaakov from Esav's bite.[430]

Moshe from Pharoah's executioner.[431]

Rav Refael ben Shmuel Meyuchas.[432]

---

430 Breshis Rabbah 78:9.
431 Devraim Rabbah 2:29.
432 Megillas Hanes Mishpachas Meyuchus.

Rejuvenation

Today, partly the result of vanity, people are doing all sorts of things to look younger again.

In past times, Hashem rejuvenated people for a holy purpose.

Sarah.[433]

Yocheved.[434]

Miriam.[435]

The Daughters of Tzelafchad.[436]

Esther.[437]

---

433 Baba Metzia 87a.
434 Baba Basra 120a.
435 Sidur Hamevoar Avir Yaakov, Haroeh Chalom.
436 Baba Basra 119b.
437 Rebbi Eliyahu Hacohen Haitmari Meizmer in Midrash Eloyahu.

Things Switched

There have been occasions when one thing was miraculously transformed to something else to assist a particular situation. There are some of the events:

The Teraphim that Rachel stole changed to plates.[438]

Water changed to Seed for Yaakov's sheep.[439]

A Staff changed to a snake.[440]

Bread changed to frogs in the plague.[441]

Water changed to blood in the plague.[442]

Soil changed to lice in the plague.[443]

---

438 Breshis Rabbah 74:9.
439 Breshis Rabbah 73:10.
440 Shmos 4:2; Vaera 7:10.
441 Zohar Vaera 29b.
442 Vaera 7:20.
443 Vaera 8:13.

Tunnels

There are many tunnels dug even in modern times. There are tunnels that have existed for millennia that have connected the most amazing places:

Between outside of Israel and Israel (for the Righteous to pass through during the times of the resurrection of the dead).[444]

Between Moshe's grave and Maarat Hamachpela.[445]

Between Maarat Hamachpela and the Kosel Hamaaravi. [446]

Between Moshe's grave and Aharon's grave and Miriam's grave.[447]

---

444 Ksuvos 111a.
445 Zohar Chukas 183a.
446 Gam Ani Odecha in the name of the Arizal.
447 Zohar Chukas 183a.

Foundation Stone (Even Shesiyah)

This stone is the point from which Hashem created the world and on which the Holy of Holies rested.[448]

There is another explanation that the stones that Yaakov put under his head, that merged to became one stone, became the Foundation Stone.[449]

We are taught that one of Hashem's holy names was written on it,[450] and there is an opinion that the 12 stones of the Choshen come from this foundation stone.[451]

---

448 Zohar Noach 71b.
449 Pirkei Derebbi Eliezer 35.
450 Targum Yonatan ben Uziel Titzaveh 28:30.
451 Alshich Tetzave 28:17.

Stones

There have been many miraculous things that have occurred with different stones. We know Yaakov had several stones under his head when he lay down and they became one.[452] Similarly when David fought Golias he picked five stones for his slingshot, and they too became one.[453]

Each of the twelve tribes in the Midbar brought their tribe's stone for the Choshen. How did they get it? Each tribe received it in their encampment accompanied with the Manna as it fell from the sky.[454]

According to one opinion the window in Noah's Ark was really a jewel that lit up the Ark. Which jewel was it? The Bareket, [455] which incidentally was the stone of Levi in the Choshen, the third one in the first row. [456]

Also interesting is that the Manna was described as appearing like the Bedolach stone.[457] And just like the Manna could taste like anything, the Bedolach stone would take on the appearance of the garment it was on. [458]

---

452 Chulin 91b.
453 Tikunei Zohar 21:62a.
454 Yalkut Yosef Yayakhel, Chizkuni Vayakhel.
455 Rabbeinu Bechaya Titzave 28:15.
456 Shmos Rabbah Tetzave 38:9.
457 Behaalosecha 11:7.
458 Imre Shefer Introduction to Vayetzei.

The Hidden Light (Ohr Haganuz)

There was a special light created during the six days of creation that was hidden in Gan Eden for the Righteous in future.[459] According to one opinion this light lasted only three days before it was hidden,[460] whereas another opinion states it lasted a week. It later came back to give light in Noach's ark,[461] and for Bnei Yisrael during the Plague of Darkness on the Mitzrim.[462] The righteous would have light to see with, and the wicked died during the three days of darkness from the power of the Ohr Haganuz.[463] The light was also said to reappear at the time of Matan Torah.[464]

An interesting fact is that it is the Ohr Haganuz that caused the Manna to turn into a physical form in this world.[465]

---

459 Maharzav on Breishis Rabbah 3:6.
460 Tana Debei Eliyahu Zuta 21.
461 Ohr Haganuz Vaeschanan.
462 Sifsei Cohen Bo.
463 Yikra Duraisa Bo in the name of Rabbi Tzvi Roteberg.
464 Targum and Rashi Chabakuk 3:3.
465 Ramban Beshalach 16:16.

Adonei Hasadeh / Avnei Hasadeh / Yadua

There is an animal called an Adonei Hasadeh or Avnei Hasadeh.[466] It is also known as the Yadua, and is connected from its navel to the ground through a long cord on which it grows, like gourds on a vine. Its appearance is like a man. No one can come close to the animal within the circumference of the cord, or it will kill you. The only way to kill it is by cutting through the cord, severing its lifeline.[467] The cord is fifty amos long,[468] and Esav was an expert in hunting this animal.[469]

The animal is created from the seed of a person. For example, sometimes shepherds lose their seed during the warm months and such seed germinates in the ground and from there grows this creature.[470] This creature was one of the animals that was in the plague of wild beasts.[471] An alternate view says the creature was like a sheep, tasted like a fish and its blood was as sweet as honey,[472] or was like a dog,[473] or was a bird.[474]

A sorcerer would take a bone from this animal and insert it into his mouth and would speak through it.[475] Balak, for example, would do so.[476]

---

466 Mishna Kilayim 8:5.

467 Sifsei Chachamim Vayikra 19:31; Rav Ovadia Mibartenura Klayim 8:5.

468 Asiris Haefah Shimini.

469 Hagra.

470 Midrash Talpiot Ov.

471 Hagra.

472 Maaseh Tuvia, Olam Hakatan 10.

473 Etz Chaim Heichal Hashvi Shaar Harishon 1.

474 Rambam Hilchos Avodah Zara 86:2.

475 Rashi Sanhedrin 65.

476 Ohr Hachaim Balak 22:41; Yalkut Reuveini Balak.

Trees that Tasted like their Fruit

Originally all the trees were supposed to taste like the fruit that grew on them, but the trees disobeyed Hashem and by and large did not taste like the fruit they bear.[477] There were exceptions though. The Etrog's tree tastes like its fruit,[478] and the Etrog is one of the four possibilities for the fruit that Adam and Chava ate.[479]The roots of the Etrog tree grow in the form of the letters of Hashem's 4 letter name.[480]

---

477 Rashi Breishis 1:11.
478 Sukkah 35a.
479 Breishis Rabbah 15:7.
480 Tzvi Letadik on the introduction to the Tikeunei Zohar.

Bilam's Donkey

Everyone knows that the Torah recorded the incident of Bilam's donkey speaking.[481] But are you aware that famous donkey was the mother of Avraham's donkey?[482] Avraham's donkey, which would eventually be ridden by Moshe and eventually by the Mashiach.[483] How did Bilam get such an important donkey? Well Yaakov gave it to him![484] One other amazing fact is that many years later Shimshon would fight off the Plishtim with the jawbone of a donkey. Yes, that jawbone was from the donkey of Bilam![485]

---

481 Balak 22:28.
482 Pirke Derebbi Eliezer 31.
483 Pirke Derebbi Eliezer 31.
484 Torah Shleima Balak 21.
485 Meom Loez Shoftim 15:15.

The Well of Miriam

Just like the Manna was food for Beni Yisrael during the forty years in the Midbar, the Well of Miriam provided them liquid nourishment. And just like Manna could taste like anything, the liquid from the Well of Miriam would taste like anything one wanted,[486] although there is another opinion that states that one could taste old wine, new wine, milk, honey and anything sweet.[487] It flowed amongst the camp like a river,[488] and around the Well grew all sort of grasses that people would roll in and become fragrant.[489] Within the water were all types of fatty fish,[490] and because of the water, each person could plant figs, grapes and pomegranates nearby and they would produce fruit in one day![491]

---

486 Midrash Talpiot Yayin.
487 Mechilte Yisro.
488 Hadar Zekeinim Chukas.
489 Midrash Shochar Tov 23.
490 Breishis Rabbah 66:3.
491 Tanchuma Kedoshim 7.

Mermaids / Mermen

Sightings of mermaids or mermen have occurred all over the world. They are a part of our culture as well, appearing in the Gemara under the name Dolphinin,[492] which is like the English word Dolphin. It is not only mentioned in the Gemara, Rashi, and Tosfos, but also in a Tosephta there. Rashi says the name in Laaz, a foreign tongue, is Sirena, which is very similar to the English word Siren. And it is described as a creature with the upper half having a human form and the bottom half the form of a fish.[493] Besides Dolphinin and Sirena it is also called a Silonis, which is very similar to the English Words 'Sea Lion.'[494] In Toras Cohanim there is difference of opinion if the word should be Silonis or Sironis.[495] Somehow it joined the other animals during the plague of wild beasts and with its arms filled with poison,[496] that were ten amos long, climbed on the roof and opened the locked doors of the Mitzrim.[497] It is said to sing to sailors at sea, which puts them to sleep and afterwards the Sironis board the boat, and kill and eat the sailors.[498]

---

492 Bechoros 8a.
493 Rashi Bechors 8a; Midbar Kadmus – Dag; Tosfos Hashalem Shmini.
494 Ramban Shmini 11:10.
495 Toras Cohanim Shmini 3:4; Raavad.
496 Midrash Agada Vaera.
497 Tosfos Hashalem Vaera 9:27; Sefer Hayashar Bo.
498 Midbar Kadmus Dag; Tosfos Hashalem Shmini.

Behemoth

Behemoth, also known as Shor Habar, is a large animal of which Hashem only created two, a male and a female. Hashem neutered the male and cooled the female,[499] otherwise they would have populated the whole world. Of all the animals that Hashem created on day six of creation, the Behemoth was the first one created.[500] There is an opinion that the meat that the angels roasted for Adam when he was in Gan Eden[501] came from the Behemoth.[502]

---

499 Baba Basra 74b.
500 Netzudas Dovid Iyov 40:19.
501 Sanhedrin 59b.
502 Midrash Talpiot Adam Harishon.

The Middle Post

In the Mishkan there were posts going through the sides of the boards that held them together and gave them stability. The middle post was miraculously put in place as it traversed one side of the Mishkan, made a ninety degree turn and traversed the other side and finally made another ninety degrees turn to traverse the third side.[503] It was seventy amos in length and came with Bnei Yisrael at Krias Yam Suf when the angels cut the trees that Yaakov replanted in Mitzrayim[504] from the trees Avraham planted in Beer Sheva for the future Mishkan.[505] There is another opinion, that states before it was used in the Mishkan it was Yaakov's walking stick.[506]

---

503 Targum Yonatan ben Uziel Trumah 26:28.
504 Breishis Rabbah 94:4.
505 Targum Yonatan ben Uziel Trumah 26:28; Rabeinu Bechaya 26:28.
506 Daas Zekeinim Mibaalei Hatosfos Teruma 25:5.

Werewolf

Hard to believe, but the phenomenon of a werewolf exists in Jewish literature. In general, only a few people can become werewolves.[507] And those people will still have a tail when they convert back to being a human.[508] They cannot convert back until they eat human blood,[509] or by spreading ashes on them.[510] The most famous werewolf we know of was Binyamin, the son of Yaakov.[511] Yaakov was able to control Binyamin to prevent him from turning into a werewolf.[512] The name "werewolf" is brought in the Sefer Chasidim,[513] but it is also called "Luf Garo",[514] very similar to "Lupus" with which we are familiar.

---

507 Tzioini Breishis.
508 Rabeynu Ephraim Vayechi.
509 Rabeinyu Ephrayim Breshis.
510 Rabeinu Ephrayim Vayechi.
511 Rabeinu Ephrayim Vayechi.
512 Rabeinu Ephraim Vayigash.
513 Sefer Chasidim 1465.
514 Rabbeinu Ephrayim Vayechi.

Dudaim (Mandrakes)

Dudaim were the fertility plants that Reuven went to get for his mother Leah when she stopped producing children.[515] Their appearance is like a man.[516] There is another opinion that it was more like a tree than a plant, and appeared like a man with a cord attached from its navel to the ground and whoever ripped it from the ground died.[517] Reuven came and tied his donkey to the tree and returned later to find the tree uprooted and the donkey dead.[518] That is because whoever hears the voice of the Dudaim as they were being cut would die.[519]

How does it grow? One opinion states that seed from Yaakov one time exited with his urine and from that they were created (similar to one opinion that the Adonei Hasadeh were created).[520] Another opinion states that it grows from the ground and after several years it becomes a live animal, appearing like a person.[521]

---

515 Vayetzei 30:14.
516 Tosfos Hashalem Vayetzei, Otzar Pleios Vayetzei.
517 Chemdas Hayamim Vayetzei.
518 Tzror Hamor Veyeitzei; Megadim Chadashim Vayetzei.
519 Tosfos Hashalem Vayetzei, Vayechi.
520 Lebinyomin Amar in the name of Mechamdei Shamayim.
521 Ruach Hachaim 79:2.

Feast for the Future

The most wonderous feast is in store for the righteous in the future world. Hashem plans the meal to include:

Behemoth, Leviathan, and the bird Ziz, which we have discussed elsewhere.[522] There will be a most unusual fight in the end of days, when the Leviathan will use its fin to slaughter the Behemoth at the same time that the Behemoth will be goring the Leviathan to death.[523] Manna will also be served at the feast.[524] What to drink? Of course, wine from the grapes of the six days of creation.[525] What will dessert be? Fruit from the Etz Hachaim,[526] and almonds from Aharon's staff.[527]

---

522 Baba Basra 74b.
523 Vayikra Rabbah 13:3.
524 Addition of the Bach on Chagigah 12b; Tiferes Tzvi on the Zohar Beshalach 62b.
525 Otzar Midrashim Seudas Gan Eden 89.
526 Ohr Olam Breishis.
527 Megadim Chadashim Korach in the name of Egra Dekallah.

Ziz

The Ziz is a huge bird,[528] that has other names such as Bar Yo-chani,[529] Ziz Shad-dai, and Tarnegol Habar.[530] The Ziz is so big that when it spreads its wings it can cover the sun, and is also described as having many tastes to it.[531]

---

528 Rashi Bechoros 57b.
529 Rabeinu Bechaya Beshalach 16:4.
530 Targum Sheni Eshter 3:7; Targum Tehillim 50:11.
531 Vayikra Rabbah 22:10.

Chol

This bird is also called an Oreshena, that Noach blessed in the Ark not to die, since it didn't bother Noach to feed it.[532] Another version has the bird called Melachem, and is blessed to live one thousand years since it did not eat from the Tree of Knowledge of Good and Evil. It then is destroyed and becomes an egg ready to hatch and start its life all over again.[533] There is another opinion as to how it rejuvenates itself. After three hundred and fifteen years it builds a nest, turns to face the sun and flaps its wings rapidly until it creates a fire in the nest, and it is consumed therein. After nine days a small worm emerges from the ashes and grows until thirty days later when it is a bird once more and restarts the cycle.[534] Sounds like the famous Phoenix.

---

532 Sanhedrin 108b.
533 Breshis Rabbah 19:5; Breshis Rabbati 24:34.
534 Midbar Kadmus Chol.

Trans

Today modern science has allowed men to physically become women and women to physically become men. But we know there is nothing new under the sun.[535] So where did this phenomenon occur before? The wife of Potifar continuously enticed Yosef to sin with her. One day, when he was about to succumb to her advances, he checked himself and found that he was no longer male![536] On the other hand, Queen Vashti refused to appear naked in front of Achashverosh and his guests. The accepted reason is that either the angel Gavriel fashioned a tail on her or that she broke out in leprosy.[537] There is another opinion though by Rav Shlomo Alkabetz, the composer of Lecha Dodi, which states that Vashti was embarrassed to come because she found herself to be a male![538] These occurrences were one time phenomenon, but there is an opinion in the animal kingdom, that a rabbit regularly changes from male to female and back again.[539]

---

535 Koheles 1:9.
536 Hadar Zekainim Vayeshev.
537 Megilla 12b.
538 Manos Halevi 1:12.
539 Even Ezra Shmini 11:3.

The Aron of Yosef

When it was time to leave Mitzrayim, Moshe wanted to keep the promise made to Yosef many years ago that Bnei Yisrael would take his bones out with them. Well, where was the aron of Yosef with the bones inside? No one knew until Serach bas Asher was asked by Moshe and she told him the casket was placed by the Mitzrim in the Nile.[540] Moshe wrote on a tablet, threw it into the Nile and up floated the casket. What was written on the tablet Moshe threw into the Nile? There are different opinions: either the special name of Hashem,[541] or a picture of an ox,[542] or both.[543] Rashi takes a different approach and states that the word "Arise Ox" were written on the tablet.[544]

Where did the tablet that Moshe threw into the Nile come from? One opinion ties the tablet to Yosef's special cup that he had secretly placed into Binyomin's sack to get the brothers to return to Mitzrayim. That cup was cut into four pieces. One had the image of a lion on it, another piece the image of an ox, another piece the image of an eagle and finally the last piece had an image of man on it. These are the famous four images of Yechezkel's vision of Hashem's chariot.[545] And one by one Moshe threw each piece into the Nile, but the casket of Yosef did not rise, until the last piece with the image of man was thrown in.[546]

What happened to the bones of Yosef? One opinion is that they stayed in the casket and traveled with Bnei Yisrael in the Midbar for 40 years.[547] The other fascinating opinion is that the bones were wrapped in a sheepskin and Yosef became a sheep and wandered with Bnei Yisrael for forty years![548]

---

540 Sotah 13a.
541 Medrash Aggadah Beshalach; Midrash Hagadol Veyechi.
542 Tanchuma Beshalach 2,
543 Pirkei Derebbi Eliezer 54.
544 Rashi Ki Tisa 32:4.
545 Yechezkel 1:10.
546 Midrash Hagadol Veyechi.
547 Tzror Hamor Bamidbar.
548 Tosfos Shantz Sotah 13a.

Unusual Creatures

Unusual creatures have been mentioned in the literature of cultures around the world. There are several texts in Judaism that also describe such creatures. Anah was said to have found the 'Yamim' in the desert. The 'Yamim" are said to be mules.[549] More interestingly, around that desert there were one hundred and twenty creatures that came to that area. Some of them from the bottom down appeared human, but from the top up appeared like bears or monkeys.[550] Tzefo the son of Eliphaz, who himself was the son of Esav, once went looking for his cow and found it being eaten by a creature whose top half looked like a human, but whose bottom half looked like an animal.[551]

There is a place beneath the ground called Arka, and it was there that descendants of Kayin lived, some having two heads.[552] And in fact Ashmodai, the chief of the demons, brought a two headed man from underground.[553] Another opinion states that the place beneath the ground called Tevel is where unusual creatures can be found. Some have the head of a lion on the body of a man, or the head of an ox on the body of a man, while others are the exact opposite. Finally, there is also the tradition of the man with two heads, four hands, one body and just two legs.[554]

---

549 Rashi Vayishlach 36:24.
550 Sefer Hayashar Vayishlach.
551 Sefer Hayashar Shmos.
552 Zohar Vayetzei 157a; Vayishlach 178a.
553 Tosfos Menachos 37a.
554 Chesed Lavraham 2:4.

Witchcraft

Witchcraft has been around forever, and there are people who claim to be practicing witches today. Although there can be charlatans, there have been real witches who have used witchcraft in history, even though witchcraft is strictly forbidden in the Torah.[555] Pharoah's sorcerers used witchcraft to change their staffs to snakes.[556] Amalek was certainly big in witchcraft and with the first war against Bnei Yisrael picked people whose birthday was that day so that astrologically they would be protected.[557] Balak was a big sorcerer who used a bird he fashioned for his magic.[558] Bilam was a famous magician who wrote a book of incantations.[559] Ben Stada secreted out magic incantations from Mitzrayim in a cut in his flesh.[560]

There are interesting properties about witchcraft. If you lift a witch off the ground, her magic won't work.[561] All magic can be stopped using water,[562] since it does not work on water.[563] It also doesn't work in the daytime when it is cloudy.[564] The best time for the big witches is from 12:30pm until 3:30pm and that is called Erev Gadol and the witches are called Erev Rav. The little witches work from 3:30pm until midnight.[565] Aside from the time of day, the day itself must be right, as for example certain witchcraft will not work on Shabbos.[566] Finally one should know that wearing linen clothes is a protection from witchcraft.[567]

---

555 Mishpatim 22:17.
556 Sanhedrin 67b.
557 Yerushalmi Rosh Hashannah 3:8.
558 Ohr Hachaim Balak 22:41.
559 Zohar Haazeinu299b.
560 Shabbos 104b.
561 Rashi Sanhedrin 44b.
562 Sanhedrin 77b.
563 Sanhedrin 67b.; Tiferes Yehonatan Breishis.
564 Tiferes Yehonasan Balak.
565 Zohar Ki Sisa 191a.
566 Sanhedrin 65b.
567 Meom Loez Yehoshua 2:6.

Babies Switched at Birth

There have been a few stories in the media over the years of nurses confusing two babies and they were switched only to be raised by the opposite family. In the Jewish tradition we have a purposeful switch even earlier than in the nursery. When Rachel and Leah were both pregnant, either Rachel[568] or Leah[569] prayed that Leah would have a girl and Rachel would have a boy, so that Rachel would not be less than Bilha and Zilpah, who already had two boys each. As it turns out Leah was carrying Yosef and Rachel was carrying Dina. However, the prayers were heard and either early in the pregnancy,[570] or right at delivery[571] the babies were switched, and so Leah delivered Dina (that Rachel had been carrying) and Rachel delivered Yosef (that Leah had been carrying). There is one final opinion that states Dina was switched with Binyomin,[572] again so Rachel would have two boys, just like Bilha and Zilpah did.

---

568 Yerushalmi Berachos 9:3.
569 Tanchuma Vayetzei 8.
570 Berachos 60a.
571 Targum Yonatan ben Uziel Vayetzei 30:21.
572 Sechel Tov 30:21.

The Throne of Shlomo

King Shlomo had a magnificent throne made of ivory and gold with six steps.[573] According to one version, the first step had a lion facing an ox, the second step had a wolf facing a sheep, the third step had a leopard facing a baby goat, the fourth step had a bear facing a deer, the fifth step had an eagle facing a bird.[574] Another version has on the first step a sheep facing a wolf, the second step had a deer facing a bear, the third step had a Yachmud facing an elephant, the fourth step had a Re'em facing a Grifit, and the fifth step had a man facing a demon. Above them a Ziz facing an eagle, and a dove facing a Netz.[575] And Shlomo would ascend the throne by having each animal pass King Shlomo to the next one.[576] The animals were made out of gold. [577]

573　Melachim 1: 10:18-20.
574　Otzar Mefarshim 527.
575　Otzar Mefarshim 528.
576　Otzar Midrashim 528.
577　Targum Sheni Esther 2.

The Luchos

There are many wondrous things connected to the tablets that had the ten commandments written on them, but we will mention only a few of them. The Luchos were made of Sapphire and nonetheless were able to be miraculously rolled up.[578] The first Luchos were written in Ashuris lettering and so had the conical inside of the letter "mem" and "samech" miraculously suspended within in.[579] The second set of Luchos were written in Ivri lettering and so it had the inside of the letter "ayin" suspended within it.[580]

Since the letters were cut all the way through the stone, there is a dispute as to how the backside of the Luchos were seen. One opinion is that the letters on the back of the Luchos were backwards.[581] Another opinion is that the letters would be miraculously forwards even on the flip side.[582] And another opinion is that miraculously on the back of the right tablet would be the writing of the left tablet, whereas on the back of the left tablet would be the writing of the right tablet.[583]

There are so many more letters on the right tablet than the left one, so the right tablet's letters were smaller than the left tablet's letters to allow each one to have the same amount of stone.[584] When the Luchos were broken each broken piece had a letter on it and there were 600,000 pieces, because there were additional words of Torah in between each letter of the Ten Commandments.[585] Another opinion states that only the canonical cylinders that were inside the "mem" and "samech" were broken.[586]

---

578 Shir Hashirim Rabbah5:14.

579 Shabbos 104.

580 Yerushalmi Megillah 1:9, Ridbaz.

581 Shabbos 104a.

582 Midrash Hagadol Ki Sisa 32:15; Malbim Ki Sisa 31:18.

583 Shvili Pinchas in the name of Arugas Habosem.

584 Pardes Yosef Ki Sisa in the name of Kovetz Dersahim; Bais Elokim 12.

585 Yerushalmi Shekalim 6:1.; Meah Keshita Teruma.

586 Megadim Chadashim Ki Sisa in the name of Agadas Eliyahu on Yerushalmi Shekalim.

אנכי ה׳
לא יהיה
לא תשא
זכור את
כבד את
לא תרצח
לא תנאף
לא תגנב
לא תענה
לא תחמד

The Luz Bone

The Luz bone is the bone from which there will be Techias Hamesim (Resurrection of the Dead).[587] It is indestructible,[588] and gets it nourishment from Melaveh Malka.[589] It is also called Neskvi,[590] or Besuel Haramah.[591] Where is it located on the human body? There is a multitude of answers. Either it is at the end of the spinal column (Kliboses),[592] or the very top of the spinal column,[593] or the place on the head one places his Head Tefillin,[594] or the small bone which is under the brain in the skull.[595]

---

587 Breishis Rabbah 28:3.

588 Vayikra Rabbah 1:18.

589 Kaf Hachaim 300: 1-2.

590 Mishna Brurah Ohr Hachaim 300:6.

591 Midrash Hanelem 1, Toldos 137.

592 Shabbos 152a; Midrash Talpiot Adam.

593 Sefer Habris 1: 11,10.

594 Zohar Noach 69a.

595 Chesed Lavraham 4:52.

The Leviathan

Hashem created this huge sea creature to sport with.[596] He made two of them and neutered the male, killed the female and salted it to be eaten in the future by the righteous.[597] The skin of the Leviathan will be used as a dwelling for the righteous,[598] although another opinion states that the skin will be used as clothing for the righteous and also spread out over the walls of Yerushalayim.[599]

It has the appearance of a human.[600] Its flesh shines more than its skin does.[601] It brings forth fire and will champion the Behemoth.[602] It eats the Shibuta fish,[603] as well as all big sea creatures.[604] It does not eat often, maybe once every Shmita or once every Yovel, and does not drink often, maybe once every seventy years.[605] One funny thing is that despite being so big, it is afraid of the small creature called Kilbas![606]

---

596 Tehillim 104:26.
597 Baba Basra 74b.
598 Baba Basra 75a.
599 Tosfos Hashalem Teruma.
600 Midrash Talpiot Chukim.
601 Toras Chaim Veyechi on Baba Basra 75a.
602 Agadah Breishis 76.
603 Baba Basra 74a.
604 Pirke Derebbi Eliezer 9.
605 Ben Yehoyada Baba Basra 75a.
606 Shabbos 77b.

The Staff of Moshe

Everyone knows about Moshe's staff, with which he performed signs for Bnei Yisrael and Pharoah. Later, of course, he used it for the plagues on Mitzraim and to split the sea. Where did this staff come from? Rabbi Levi says it was created right before Hashem rested on the seventh day. It was given to Adam and then subsequently passed down through the generations to Chanoch, Noach, Shem, Avraham, Yitzchak, Yaakov and finally Yosef. From Pharoah's palace, Yisro later took it and planted it in his garden, where no one could approach it until Moshe came and was able to pull it out.[607] Anyone else who approached it would be swallowed up.[608] Maybe that's where the idea of King Arthur and the Sword in the Stone came from!

What was the staff made of? Some say it was from the Tree of Knowledge of Good and Evil, and that after Moshe hit the rock and repented, he was given a staff from the Tree of life.[609] Others say it was made of sapphire and weighted forty Saah.[610] If it was wood based it was the piece of wood Moshe threw in the bitter waters to sweeten them.[611] And later, the twelve Spies used it to protect themselves from the Giants.[612]

There are many opinions as to what was written on it. Some say either the name of Hashem, the ten plagues, Avraham, Yitchak, Yaakov, Sarah, Rivka Rachel, Leah, Bilha, Zilpa, and the twelve tribes,[613] or the seventy names of Hashem.[614] Others say it was a square rod with one side having engraved on it Dtzach, Adash, Beachav, another side had the name of Hashem. It was that side that split the sea, another side hit the rock, and the fourth side was for taking the water out of the rock years later.[615] Another opinion states that on one side was engraved a

607 Pirkei Derebbi Eliezer 40.
608 Midrash Vayosha on Azi Vezimras Ya.
609 Yalkut Reuveini Chukat.
610 Shmos Rabbah 8:3.
611 Zohar Beshalach 60b.
612 Zohar Shelach 160a.
613 Targum Yonatan ben Uziel Beshalach 14:21
614 Yalkut Shimoni Beshalach 264.
615 Zohar Beshalach 48a.

snake, another side had Hashem's 72 letter name on it, another side had Hashem's 4 letter name and the last side had Dtzach, Adash, Beachav on it.[616] Finally there is also an opinion that each side had one letter of Hashem's four letter name engraved on it.[617]

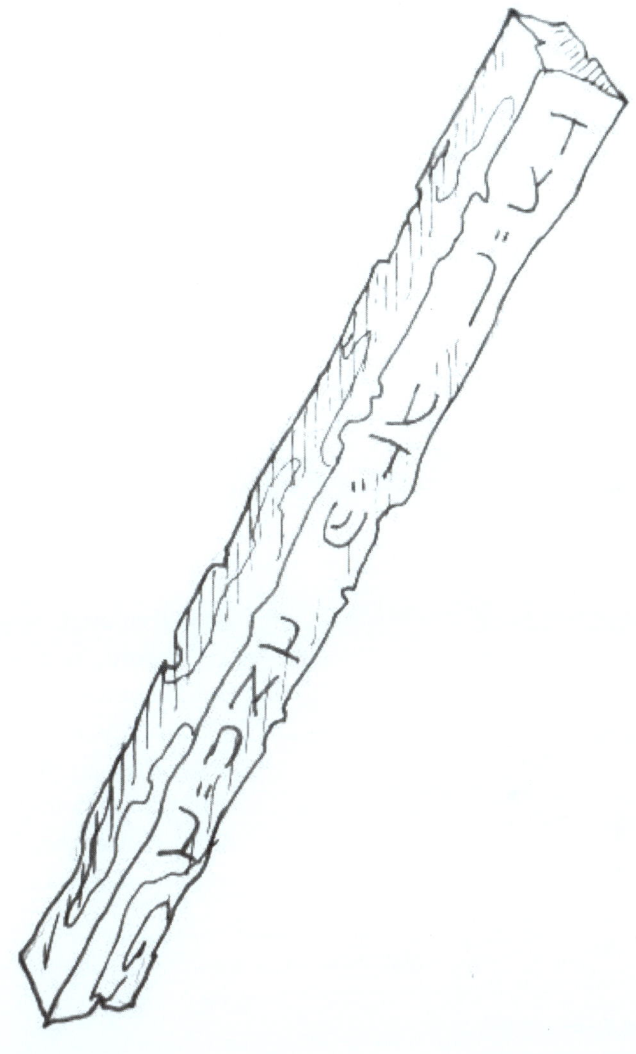

616 Zohar Beshalach 48a.
617 Tiferes Tzvi on Zohar Vaera 28.

Manna

Manna, as we all know, could taste like anything one wanted it to.[618] According to one opinion this was only after Matan Torah.[619] And another opinion states that they could only taste foods that were known to them.[620] And yet another opinion states it had 546 tastes, which is the gematria of the word sweet (Matok).[621] Yona and the fish that swallowed him both ate leftover Manna.[622] It was absorbed into the limbs of whoever ate it without forming any waste.[623] Interestingly, whoever ate from it didn't feel hungry anymore more, nor were they satisfied.[624] Another opinion states that it had the same texture as the actual food.[625] The most amazing thing about it was that it was so spiritual it went down the windpipe instead of the food pipe![626]

It also had its appearance change to all the colors of the world,[627] although on Shabbos it was white.[628] It had a fragrance like all the foods in the world,[629] whereas another opinion is that it was so fragrant, women did not need different types of perfume.[630] Along with the Manna, precious gems, women's jewelry,[631] and clothing descended.[632]

---

618 Mechilte Yisro, Vayishma Yisro.
619 Mishulchan Rebbi Eliyahu Boruch Behalosecha.
620 Kedushas Levi Behalosecha.
621 Yalkut Shimoni Shir Hashirim 986.
622 Rashi Yonah 2:1.
623 Yoma 75b.
624 Yomas 74b.
625 Yuma 75a.
626 Ketzipehcas Dvash 93 in the name of Menachem Tzion Vayetzei.
627 Ketzipechas Dvash 31 in the name of Menachem Tzion 106; Chemdas Yamim Behaalosecha.
628 Malbim Beshalach 31.
629 Klei Yakar Beshalach 16:15.
630 Sifre Behalosecha 89.
631 Yuma 75a.
632 Tosfos Hashalem Beshalach 16:19.

The Salamander

The creature we know as a salamander is obviously different from the one that is the Talmud, which is described as originating in fire.[633] There are different insights as to how it was created. We are told that it comes from fire that has been continuously burning for seven years,[634] or seven days.[635] The fire is started by burning Hadas (myrtle) branches using witchcraft.[636] The most amazing thing is that it is a fire retardant for living creatures, so that if someone smears the blood of a salamander on him, he will not get burned.[637] Chizkiyahu was saved from fire by being smeared with salamander blood.[638]

---

633 Chagigah 27a.
634 Rashi Chagigah 27a.
635 Tanchumah Vayeshev 3.
636 Rashi Chullin 127a.
637 Tanchumah Vayeshev 3; Ben Yehoyada Chagigah 27a.
638 Sanhedrin 63b.

Sefer Yetzirah

Sefer Yetzirah is an ancient Hebrew text, written by Avraham and then passed down to Yitzchak, then to Yaakov, and then to his prominent children.[639] The text gives various methods to manipulate the letters of the Holy Language of Hebrew to create certain things. People have been created with the book, such as Avraham who created beings,[640] the tribes who created women with whom they would stroll,[641] Yirmiyahu and his son Sira created a person,[642] and finally Rava also did so.[643]

Animals have also been created with the Sefer Yetzirah. The tribes did so,[644] Avraham did so, creating cattle to feed the angels,[645] and finally Rav Chanina and Rav Oyshaya created a 'third born' calf.[646]

There are certain qualities to these creations. They cannot speak,[647] and cannot hear.[648] One can only create such creatures on Friday, because animals were created on the sixth day.[649] These creatures only exist for 24 hours,[650] and the meat of the animals doesn't satisfy.[651]

One is not supposed to use the Sefer Yetzirah when he is by himself,[652] and it is forbidden to use the sefer if you are not yet twenty years old.[653] If one writes the formula of the Hebrew letters used to make the creature backwards, the creature returns to become dirt again.[654]

639　Shlah Veyeishev.
640　Rokeach Lech Lecha.
641　Shlah Veyeshev.
642　Yalkut Reuveini Breshis.
643　Sanhedrin 65b.
644　Shlah Vayeshiv.
645　Chesed Lavraham 5:51.
646　Sanhedrin 65b.
647　Sanhedrin 65b.
648　Megadim Chadashim Berachos 139 in the name of Shealas Yaavetz 2:82.
649　Rashba Sanhedrin 65b.
650　Ben Yehoyada Sanhedrin 65b.
651　Ben Yehoyada Sanhedrin 65b.
652　Yalkut Reuveini Bresihis.
653　Kesef Nivchar Vayeshev in the name of the Ramak.
654　Yalkut Reuveini Breishis.

The Golden Calf

The golden calf made after Moshe went up to Har Sinai didn't appear only as a species of cow. The front half was like an ox, but the bottom half was like a donkey![655] Some say it had two faces – that of an ox and that of a donkey.[656] The Golden Calf spoke up and said, "I am the Lord your G-d".[657] It also said, "the mixed multitude" (Erev Raav) made me.[658]

---

655 Yalkut Reuveini Ki Sisa.
656 Matuk Midvash Tikunei Zohar 142a.
657 Yalkut Reuveint Ki Sisa.
658 Tosfos Hashalem Ki Sisa 32:11; Ohr Hachaim Ki Sisa 32:19.

Unusual Birds

There is a tree on the coast of England on which birds grow from it, connected to it through their mouth. When grown, it drops off the tree into the water and moves about.[659] Another version states that there are geese growing on the trees in Ireland, and when they are ready they drop off the tree into the water and grow there.[660] These birds, according to one opinion, were the Slav birds that Hashem sent to Bnei Yisrael when they were in the Midbar.[661]

A bird called the Nesher, at the age of ten, will fly towards the sun, be burned, fall into the water, and start its life over again. After ten such epochs, at age one hundred, it gets close to the sun, falls into the water, and dies.[662]

There are birds that can, by seeing each other with intent, conceive and give birth.[663] One such bird is the ostrich.[664] Another bird, called the Reeh, can look at its eggs and they will hatch.[665] And yet other birds produce offspring by just hugging one another.[666]

There is a bird that lives by the sea named the Krum. When the sun shines on it, it's plumage changes to many colors.[667] Another bird lives by the sea, called the Kik, which has oil produced from its fat.[668] There is a bird called the Zemirah that sings in the summer without stopping until its belly explodes and dies.[669] Melachem is the name of a bird that refused to eat from the Tree of Knowledge of Good and Evil, so Hashem allows it to live until one thousand and then it decreases in size to a chick and grows new feathers and restarts its life again.[670] All of the

660 Sefer Habris 11:4.
661 Rav Chaim Paltiel Behalosecha 11:31.
662 Toldos Yitzchak Breishis.
663 Yalkut Dovid Shmini.
664 Sefer Habris 14:5.
665 Pardes Yosef Reeh in the name of Yitav Panim on the Holidays.
666 Rabbeinu Bechai Tazria 12:2.
667 Berachos 6b.
668 Sechel Tov Beshalach 16.
669 Shevet Musar 22.
670 Breshis Rabati 24:34.

birds that came out of Noah's ark kept to their own kind thereafter except the bird called Sushlami.[671] In addition, there is a bird called the Netz, which every year sheds its feathers (notzosav).[672]

---

671 Sanhedrin 108a.
672 Bais Tefilla 20.

The Heavenly Clouds

The heavenly clouds (Annanei Kavod) followed Bnei Yisrael in the Midbar. They had wondrous properties. For example, they would clean the clothes of Bnei Yisrael.[673] They would flatten the mountains, raise the valleys, kill the snakes and scorpions, provide light for them and follow behind them if they left the encampment.[674] They were the transport system for Bnei Yisrael to bring them where they wanted to go.[675] Similarly if a person had a load and no animal to move it, the heavenly clouds would do the service.[676] It was an amazing 'force field" in that it would repel arrows or projectiles that the Mitzrim would throw at them.[677] It was like a CAT scanner of today, in that the heavenly clouds would allow someone to see what was inside a container without opening it up.[678] It would allow Bnei Yisrael, that were inside the heavenly clouds, to see what is outside, but people outside such as Bilam, could not see what was inside.[679] When Bnei Yisrael would see the heavenly cloud redden they would know that sun was setting, and if it whitened they would know it was shining.[680]

All these wonderous properties only occurred if Bnei Yisrael kept the Torah. If they sinned, the heavenly clouds would spit them outside of the camp.[681] And as unbelievable as it may seem, the whole tribe of Dan was outside of the camp, because they were involved in idol worship with Pesel Micha.[682] Those who were impure were also spit out of the camp.[683] When Bnei Yisrael followed the word of Hashem, the heavenly clouds formed the letter 'Chaf" in the sky, and when they didn't follow the word of Hashem, they formed the letter 'Samech"

---

673 Shir Hashirim Rabbah 4:11.
674 Sifre Behalosecha.
675 Sifsei Cohen Ekev.
676 Tanchuma Bamidbar 12.
677 Rashi Yisro 19:4.
678 Tosfos Shabbos 22b.
679 Baal Haturim Balak 22:5.
680 Midrash Aggada Pekudei.
681 Rashi, Klei Yakar, Rabeinu Bechai Ki Tetzei 25:18.
682 Tanchuma Ki Teitzei 10.
683 Pirekei Derebbi Eliezer 44.

in the sky.[684] Others say the heavenly clouds always formed the letter "Heh' in the sky.[685]

684 Rabeinu Bechai Beshalach 17:16.
685 Chizkuni Bamidbar 2:2; Rokeach Behalosecha 9:17; Tosfos Hashalem Pekudei 40:20.

The Tree of Knowledge of Good and Evil

There is basically a four-way dispute as to the exact fruit that Adam and Chava ate from this tree. The basic choices are grapes, figs, wheat, or an Etrog.[686] There are other opinions that list only a few of the 4 choices. And there is another opinion that the tree was its own kind, having nothing to do with what we know today,[687] or was a combination of all of the seven special species (wheat, barley, grape, fig, pomegranate, olive and date).[688] One other thing about this tree is that the wood – the trunk and branches – were edible and tasted like the fruit.[689]

Other amazing things about this tree include the fact that when Adam was banished from Gan Eden, the tree that he sinned from was also banished from Gan Eden and Noach brought that tree on the Ark.[690] In addition, on Moshe's last day of life he miraculously wrote thirteen Torahs and the instrument he used to write with came from this tree.[691] There is also an opinion that the gallows used to hang Haman came from this tree.[692]

---

686 Breishis Rabbah 15:17.
687 Shivtei-Kah Masai from Rav Moshe Dovid Vallei.
688 Tikunei Zohar 24:69a.
689 Sukkah 35a.
690 Yalkut Reuveini Breishis.
691 Otzar Midrashim 371.
692 Midrash Talpios Achashverosh.

Unusual Animals

Everyone loves elephants, as they are so unusual in appearance. They and monkeys are the two animals we are familiar with that one is supposed to make a Bracha upon seeing them.[693] Why? One reason given is that during the Dispersion (Tower of Babel), as a punishment, the wicked people who wanted to ascend to the sky and fight Hashem, were changed into monkeys[694] and elephants.[695] Another opinion states that during the time of the Dor HaMabul (Flood), the wicked people who wanted to ascend to the sky, and worship their G-d there, were turned into monkeys and elephants.[696] Most interesting is that unlike other animals, the mammary glands of monkeys and elephants are located in the upper chest, just like in humans!

There is a mouse that develops from the ground and in the process, it will be half mouse and half earth.[697]

The Achashtranim, mentioned in the book of Esther,[698] looked like a two humped camel,[699] and were fast animals that had eight legs. They would run on four legs, and after they would tire, those four legs would rest and they would run on the other four legs.[700]

---

693 Berachos 58b.
694 Sanhedrin 109a.
695 Sefer Hayashar Noach.
696 Maleches Shlomo Kilayim 8:6.
697 Mishnayos Chullin 9:6, Rashi Chullin 126b.
698 Esther 8:10.
699 Yaavetz Megila 18a.
700 Rokeach Breishis 2:25.

The Tzitz

The Tzitz was the golden headband worn by the Kohen Gadol. It had the word 'Kodesh LaHashem' on it, and was used to forgive sins involving brazenness.[701] It worked whether the Kohen Gadol was wearing it or not according to one opinion.[702] According to one opinion the names of the twelve tribes were also written on the Tzitz.[703] When the Tzitz was shown to the Midianites or Bilam, who used witchcraft to escape and fly away, they fell to the ground.[704]

---

701 Zevachim 88b.
702 Yuma 7b.
703 Targum Shir Hashirim 5:14.
704 Tanchuma Matos 4; Bamidbar Rabbah 22:5.

Re'emim

The Re'em is a magnificent creature, of which Hashem created two in the beginning of time. It is a kosher animal. One animal went to the east, and one went to the west. Once every seventy years the animals meet to mate, and remarkably after they mate the female kills the male. Gestation takes place over 12 months. In the eleventh month the Re'em is already so big that she can't walk, and so Hashem provides food and drink for her to eat. After 12 months her abdomen opens and she gives birth to a male and female, and one goes to the east, and one goes to the west, and she herself dies.[705]

How did the Re'em survive the Mabul (flood) if it was so big? Rebbi Yehuda says that the Re'em's cubs went on board the Ark, whereas Rebbi Nechemia says Noach tied it to the outside of the ark and it was saved.[706] It is the Dishon that is listed as one of the seven kosher wild animals,[707] and is also called an Urzila,[708] of which the size of a one day old cub was as large as Mount Tavor.[709] It has also been described as having the most beautiful horns, but it is not a very strong animal.[710]

---

705 Midbar Kadmus Karnei Re'emim; Breishis Rabbati 1, 20-23.
706 Breishis Rabbah 31:13.
707 Targum Onkelos Reeh 14:5.
708 Rashi Baba Basra 73b.
709 Baba Basra 73b.
710 Rashi Zos Habracha 33:17.

Shabbos

Shabbos is the wonderful day of rest Hashem gave us, but we are not the only things that rest on Shabbos. There is the famous river called Sambaton, that instead of flowing with water flows with stones, and it rests on Shabbos. Necromancers who raise the dead can not do so on Shabbos.[711] A mountain that is mined for silver will not produce silver on Shabbos, and the fish called Shabtei (Shibuta) leaves the water and rests on dry land on Shabbos.[712] The fires of Gehenom are supposed to be cooled on Shabbos, except for those that violated Shabbos and Yom Tov when they were alive.[713] The dove will not eat produce that was picked on Shabbos.[714] The worm will not rule the dead on Shabbos.[715] Neither Satan nor damaging spirits will rule on Shabbos.[716] There are springs of water that have no flow on Shabbos.[717] The plagues did not operate in Mitzrayim on Shabbos.[718] There was a heavenly cloud above the Aron in the Midbar and during the week the two letters of Hashem's name "yud" and "heh" would travel back and forth among the four flags of the tribes situated on each side of the camp. On Shabbos the letters did not move from where they were just before Shabbos began.[719]

---

711 Breishis Rabbah 11:5, Rashi Sanhedrin 65b.

712 Yalkut Reuveini Breshis.

713 Tiferes Tzvi on the Zohar Breishis 48a.

714 Migdal Oz, Beis Midos Aliyas Hatevah.

715 Baal Haturim Beshalach 16:24.

716 Midrash Tehillim 92.

717 Sefer Habris 1:8; Seder Hadoros Rabbi Yehuda Hanasi 12.

718 Kemotzei Shalal Rav Bo in the name of the Pnei Yehoshua.

719 Yalkut Reuveini Bamidbar.

Shibuta

The Shibuta fish is the famous fish that rest on Shabbos, and has the letters of Shabbos in its name.[720] It tastes like a pig. Some say this refers to its brain, and some say this refers to its tongue.[721] When Bnei Yisrael returned to Eretz Yisrael with Ezra, all the indigenous fish returned except the Shibuta fish.[722] It is called the Goat of the Sea.[723] It has horns and is food for the Leviathan.[724] Eating the Shibuta fish in the month of Nisan will cause tzaraas.[725] It does have amazing protective qualities, as someone who wears a skin from the Shibuta fish will be protected from arrows and spears penetrating him.[726]

---

720 Yalkut Reuveini Breishis.
721 Yalkut Shimoni Shmini 536.
722 Yerushalmi Taanis 4:5.
723 Tosfos Avoda Zara 39a.
724 Baba Basra 74a.
725 Pesachim 112b.
726 Otzar Plios in the name of Shevet Musar 11.

Slav

There is a difference of opinion as to what Slav tastes like. One opinion states that it could taste like anything you wanted, except the Leviathan.[727] Another opinion states it could taste like any meat you wanted,[728] and still another opinion states it would taste like a mixture of meat and fish.[729] The first time it came down from the heavens with the Manna, and therefore did not require Shechita.[730] It was said that the bird that grows attached to a tree, and when fully grown falls into the water, is the Slav.[731] However another source states that it is a type of fish that comes out of the water in the summer.[732]

---

727 Rokeach 31:20; Baal Haturim 31:20.
728 Sifsei Cohen Behaalosecha.
729 Chizkuni Behaalosecah 11:31.
730 Sifsei Cohen Behaalosecha.
731 Rav Cahim Paltiel Behaalosecha 11:31.
732 Maor Haafeila Beshalach.

Shamir

The Shamir was a worm-like creature that Moshe used to write the letters on the Stones of the Ephod and Choshen. He would write on them in ink and the Shamir would crawl over the ink and split the stones accordingly.[733] Its size was like a barley seed, and it would cut the stone with its nails.[734] The Nesher (eagle), or Duchifas (Ziz) brought the Shamir from Gan Eden.[735] Later on King Shlomo used the demon Ashmadai to bring the Shamir.[736]

---

733 Sotah 48b.
734 Maor Haaphela Titzaveh.
735 Midrash Tehillim 78; Chulin 63a.
736 Gittin 68b.

Tachash

The Tachash, whose hide was used as a covering for the Mishkan, was a kosher wild animal with one horn and six colors on its skin. It was created only for that time and was later hidden.[737] Some claim it is named Glacktinun or Teinun after its color, or Keresh.[738] And even though we quoted a source saying that it was kosher and had six colors, that is in dispute, as there is an opinion that it was not kosher.[739] There is also an opinion that it had seven hundred and eight colors, like its gematria.[740] There is also an opinion that perhaps the Tachash made an earlier appearance, and was the source of the clothing that Hashem fashioned for Adam and Chava.[741]

---

737 Tanchuma Teruma 6.
738 Yerushalmi Shabbos 2:3.
739 Yerushalmi Berachos 2:3.
740 Chemdas Hayamim Hatemani.
741 Rabeinu Bechaya Breishis.

Terafim

The Terafim were the idols used by Lavan, mentioned in the Torah, that Rachel stole so they would not reveal to Lavan that Yaakov and his family had run away.[742] He was not the only one who had Terafim. Micha had them,[743] and interestingly Michal had a set, but not for idol worship.[744] How are they made? One must slay a firstborn man, salt the head with salt and oil, write on a golden plate an unholy name, and place it under the tongue of the head. Place it in the wall, light candles in front of it, bow down to it, and it will respond.[745] There is another opinion that is not as gruesome. The Terafim are a copper utensil made to know time, or something that is used to for the constellations, and they speak to the person.[746]

---

742 Vayetzei 31:19.
743 Shoftim 17:5.
744 Shmuel 1, 19, 13.
745 Pirkei Derebbi Eliezer 36; Tanchuma Vaeyetzei 12, Seder Hadoros 2205.
746 Toldos Yitzchak Vayetzei.

Krias Yam Suf (Splitting of the Sea)

The splitting of the sea for Bnei Yisrael, while being chased by the Mitzrim, is a miraculous event given the scope of what happened and the perfect timing. However, there were additional fantastic things that occurred aside from Bnei Yisrael being saved on dry land and the Mitzrim being drowned. Meom Loez in Beshalach lists fifty miracles that occurred at the time of Kriyas Yam Suf. It would be impossible to have a sefer discussing wonders in the world of Torah without mentioning a few items. A few amazing wonders pertaining to the water:

1. All the waters in the world split that day![747]
2. The Yam Suf split into 12 lanes.[748]
3. Bnei Yisrael also had an arch of water over them.[749]
4. The walls of the lanes between the tribes were like sapphire and diamond and the different tribes could see each other as they went through.[750]
5. There were fruit trees on each side of the lanes that they could pick from.[751]

---

747 Shmos Rabbah 21:6.
748 Shmos Rabbah 24:1.
749 Tanchuma Beshalach 17.
750 Radal on Pikrei Derebbi Eliezer 42.
751 Shmos Rabbah 21:10.

The Ten Plagues

Nothing can be written about wonders in the world of Torah without mentioning the ten plagues. The basic description is in the Torah, and whole books have been written about the plagues. Let us at least give a cursory rendition of some of the miraculous things that occurred in Miztrayim during that time.

Blood – even the juice squeezed out of a fruit turned to blood.[752]

Frogs – at the end of the plague, the frogs died, except the ones who were willing to sacrifice themselves and entered the ovens of the Mitzrim. Those frogs lived.[753]

Lice – it was accompanied with worms and mosquitoes,[754] or fleas.[755]

Wild Beasts – even the Adonei Hasadeh, that is attached from its navel to the ground, cut out some dirt around its attachment and came with it for the plague.[756]

Pestilence – the son of Shulamis bas Dibri, who was raped by the Mitzri, was considered a Mitzri before Matan Torah, so his animals died. Pharoah thought he was considered Jewish and nonetheless his animals died, so he hardened his heart.[757]

Boils – These stayed on the Magicians of Mitzrayim until the day they died.[758]

Hail – After falling on Mitzrayim, it stayed suspended in air for 41 years, until Yehoshua's war at Beit Choron, and will come down again in the war of Gog and Magog.[759]

Locusts – When they were removed, even the dead ones that the Mitzrim salted to eat flew out of the barrels![760]

---

752 Midrash Hagadol Vaera 7:19.

753 Daas Zekainim Mibaalei Hatosfos Vaera 8:9; Yalkut Shimoni Vaera 182.

754 The Gra.

755 Rashbam Vaera 8:11.

756 Kol Eliyahu by the Gra.

757 Yalkut Shimoni Emor 657; Hagra.

758 Yalkut Shimoni Vaera 184.

759 Midrash Hagadol 9:33.

760 Shmos Rabbah 13:7.

Darkness – Although the Mitzrim could not see, there was light for the Jews, who went into the homes of the Mitzrim, and found their silver and gold, which they asked for later when the Jews left Mitzrayim.[761]

Firstborn – They were to die at midnight. Well of course midnight is a different point in time depending on which time zone you are in. Miraculously they all died precisely at their midnight, as the ones in the eastern part of Mitzrayim died first, and as a wave, the death spread westward to kill the firstborn as midnight occurred.[762]

---

761 Midrash Rabbah 14:3.
762 Chidushei Maharil Diskin Bo 12:12.

Fire and Water Together

How can two opposing entities, fire and water, be mixed together and both coexist? That is a most amazing thing, and here are some examples:

Hail in Mitzrayim.[763]

The sky itself.[764]

The upper firmament of water and the stars of fire.[765]

An Angel.[766]

A Rainbow.[767]

On Har Sinai at the time of the giving of the Torah.[768]

---

763 Vaera 9:24.
764 Rashi Breishis 1:8.
765 Yerushalmi Rosh Hashanah 2:4.
766 Yerushalmi Rosh Hashanah 2:4.
767 Machane Dan Noach in the name of the Riva.
768 Meom Loez Yisro sixth miracle.

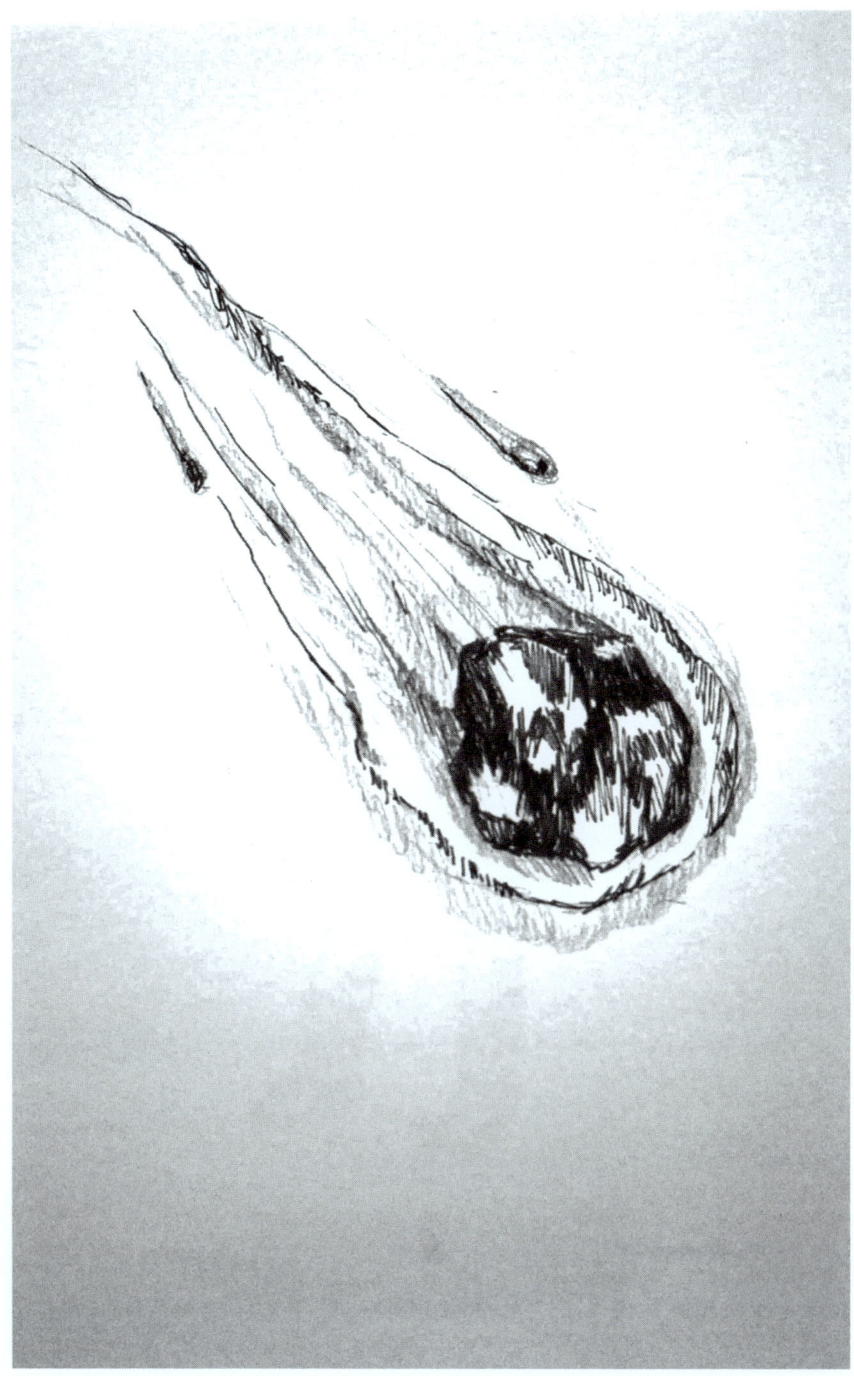

600,000 letters in the Torah

This famous saying is also hinted at in many Seforim, with the first word of the Torah, Breishis and the last word in the Torah, Yisrael – which will spell it out by anagram.[769] And corresponding to that are the 600,000 primary souls of Bnei Yisrael. The problem of course is we have only 304,805 letters in our Sefer Torah. So why are we told that there are 600,000 letters? There are many answers:

1. The number includes the full spelling of each letter, Aleph etc.[770]

2. The number includes the Targum.[771]

3. The number includes the written and vocalized text.[772]

4. The number includes the small letters (e.g. Vav and Yud), that a Sofer uses to write the letters.[773]

5. The number includes the letters that would appear from vowels.[774]

6. The number includes the hidden letters that were hidden with the Ohr Haganuz.[775]

7. The number represents the number of "Yudin" in each letter.[776]

8. The number includes the letters of the Torah Shel Baal Peh.[777]

9. The number includes the spaces on the parchment.[778]

10. The number includes hidden letters on the parchment.[779]

11. The number refers to the Sefer Torah in the Sky.[780]

---

769 Kriyas Sefer Bamidbar.
770 Zohar Chadash Shir Hashirim 91a; Chesed Leavraham Mayan Sheini, Nahar 11.
771 Pnei Yehoshua Kidushin 30a.
772 Pnei Yehoshua Kidushin 30a.
773 Pri Hatzadik Shmos.
774 Likutei Torah Baal Hatanya Behar 43b.
775 Midbar Kadmus 10.
776 Emes Leyaakov Sof Hamikra.
777 Ayeles Hashachar Pinchas 26.
778 Nitzutzei Hatorah Haazeinu in the name of Midbaros Kadsho Lag Baomer.
779 Nitzutzei Hatorah Haazeinu in the name of Chodesh Bchadsho; Maamad Hanivchar 727 in the name of the Maharsham.
780 Midrash Talpiot Osios.

12. The number refers to the time before the Luchos were broken.[781]
13. The number includes the Sefer of "Vayehi Binsoah Haaron…" and was hidden.[782]

781 Maamar Hanefesh 3:6 by Rav Menachem Azaria Mipano.
782 Midrash Mishlei 26.